C#AND SQL
CLIENT

Working with the Datatable

Richard Thomas Edwards

CONTENTS

WHY IS THE CODE BROKEN INTO SECTIONS?

This book is really condensed

T HIS BOOK IS REALL A HUGE BOOK! It just doesn't look that way if you're looking at just the length of it. For example, if you were to eliminate the stylesheets, there are approximately 68 pages before I added one – just one – example of a complete code example. In-other-words, 6 pages of one code example is almost 10 percent of this book. Imagine what 5760 would look like at just 5 pages each! This book would wind up being 28800 pages in length.

Yet, it is, indeed, all here!

```
string cnstr = "";
string strQuery = "";

System.Data.SQLClient.SQLConnection cn = new
System.Data.SQLClient.SQLConnection(cnstr);
cn.Open();

System.Data.SQLClient.SQLCommand cmd = new
System.Data.SQLClient.SQLCommand();
cmd.Connection = cn;
cmd.CommandType = 1;
cmd.CommandText = strQuery;
cmd.ExecuteNonquery();
```

```
System.Data.SQLClient.SQLDataAdapter da = new
System.Data.SQLClient.SQLDataAdapter(cmd);

System.Data.DataTable ds as new System.Data.Dataset();
da.Fill(dt);

    Scripting.FileSystemObject fso = new Scripting.FileSystemObject();
    Scripting.TextStream txtstream = fso.OpenTextFile(Application.StartupPath +
"\\Products.html",IOMode.ForWriting, True, Tristate.TristateUseDefault);
    txtstream.WriteLine("<html>");
    txtstream.WriteLine("<head>");
    txtstream.WriteLine("<title>Products</title>");
    txtstream.WriteLine("<style type='text/css'>");
    txtstream.WriteLine("body");
    txtstream.WriteLine("{");
    txtstream.WriteLine("    PADDING-RIGHT: 0px;");
    txtstream.WriteLine("    PADDING-LEFT: 0px;");
    txtstream.WriteLine("    PADDING-BOTTOM: 0px;");
    txtstream.WriteLine("    MARGIN: 0px;");
    txtstream.WriteLine("    COLOR: #333;");
    txtstream.WriteLine("    PADDING-TOP: 0px;");
    txtstream.WriteLine("    FONT-FAMILY: verdana, arial, helvetica, sans-serif;");
    txtstream.WriteLine("}");
    txtstream.WriteLine("table");
    txtstream.WriteLine("{");
    txtstream.WriteLine("    BORDER-RIGHT: #999999 1px solid;");
    txtstream.WriteLine("    PADDING-RIGHT: 1px;");
    txtstream.WriteLine("    PADDING-LEFT: 1px;");
    txtstream.WriteLine("    PADDING-BOTTOM: 1px;");
    txtstream.WriteLine("    LINE-HEIGHT: 8px;");
    txtstream.WriteLine("    PADDING-TOP: 1px;");
    txtstream.WriteLine("    BORDER-BOTTOM: #999 1px solid;");
    txtstream.WriteLine("    BACKGROUND-COLOR: #eeeeee;");
    txtstream.WriteLine("
filter:progid:DXImageTransform.Microsoft.Shadow(color='silver', Direction=135,
Strength=16)");
    txtstream.WriteLine("}");
    txtstream.WriteLine("th");
    txtstream.WriteLine("{");
    txtstream.WriteLine("    BORDER-RIGHT: #999999 3px solid;");
    txtstream.WriteLine("    PADDING-RIGHT: 6px;");
    txtstream.WriteLine("    PADDING-LEFT: 6px;");
    txtstream.WriteLine("    FONT-WEIGHT: Bold;");
    txtstream.WriteLine("    FONT-SIZE: 14px;");
    txtstream.WriteLine("    PADDING-BOTTOM: 6px;");
    txtstream.WriteLine("    COLOR: darkred;");
    txtstream.WriteLine("    LINE-HEIGHT: 14px;");
    txtstream.WriteLine("    PADDING-TOP: 6px;");
    txtstream.WriteLine("    BORDER-BOTTOM: #999 1px solid;");
    txtstream.WriteLine("    BACKGROUND-COLOR: #eeeeee;");
```

```
txtstream.WriteLine("    FONT-FAMILY: font-family: Cambria, serif;");
txtstream.WriteLine("    FONT-SIZE: 12px;");
txtstream.WriteLine("    text-align: left;");
txtstream.WriteLine("    white-Space: nowrap='nowrap';");
txtstream.WriteLine("}");
txtstream.WriteLine(".th");
txtstream.WriteLine("{");
txtstream.WriteLine("    BORDER-RIGHT: #999999 2px solid;");
txtstream.WriteLine("    PADDING-RIGHT: 6px;");
txtstream.WriteLine("    PADDING-LEFT: 6px;");
txtstream.WriteLine("    FONT-WEIGHT: Bold;");
txtstream.WriteLine("    PADDING-BOTTOM: 6px;");
txtstream.WriteLine("    COLOR: black;");
txtstream.WriteLine("    PADDING-TOP: 6px;");
txtstream.WriteLine("    BORDER-BOTTOM: #999 2px solid;");
txtstream.WriteLine("    BACKGROUND-COLOR: #eeeeee;");
txtstream.WriteLine("    FONT-FAMILY: font-family: Cambria, serif;");
txtstream.WriteLine("    FONT-SIZE: 10px;");
txtstream.WriteLine("    text-align: right;");
txtstream.WriteLine("    white-Space: nowrap='nowrap';");
txtstream.WriteLine("}");
txtstream.WriteLine("td");
txtstream.WriteLine("{");
txtstream.WriteLine("    BORDER-RIGHT: #999999 3px solid;");
txtstream.WriteLine("    PADDING-RIGHT: 6px;");
txtstream.WriteLine("    PADDING-LEFT: 6px;");
txtstream.WriteLine("    FONT-WEIGHT: Normal;");
txtstream.WriteLine("    PADDING-BOTTOM: 6px;");
txtstream.WriteLine("    COLOR: navy;");
txtstream.WriteLine("    LINE-HEIGHT: 14px;");
txtstream.WriteLine("    PADDING-TOP: 6px;");
txtstream.WriteLine("    BORDER-BOTTOM: #999 1px solid;");
txtstream.WriteLine("    BACKGROUND-COLOR: #eeeeee;");
txtstream.WriteLine("    FONT-FAMILY: font-family: Cambria, serif;");
txtstream.WriteLine("    FONT-SIZE: 12px;");
txtstream.WriteLine("    text-align: left;");
txtstream.WriteLine("    white-Space: nowrap='nowrap';");
txtstream.WriteLine("}");
txtstream.WriteLine("div");
txtstream.WriteLine("{");
txtstream.WriteLine("    BORDER-RIGHT: #999999 3px solid;");
txtstream.WriteLine("    PADDING-RIGHT: 6px;");
txtstream.WriteLine("    PADDING-LEFT: 6px;");
txtstream.WriteLine("    FONT-WEIGHT: Normal;");
txtstream.WriteLine("    PADDING-BOTTOM: 6px;");
txtstream.WriteLine("    COLOR: white;");
txtstream.WriteLine("    PADDING-TOP: 6px;");
txtstream.WriteLine("    BORDER-BOTTOM: #999 1px solid;");
txtstream.WriteLine("    BACKGROUND-COLOR: navy;");
txtstream.WriteLine("    FONT-FAMILY: font-family: Cambria, serif;");
```

```
txtstream.WriteLine("    FONT-SIZE: 10px;");
txtstream.WriteLine("    text-align: left;");
txtstream.WriteLine("    white-Space: nowrap='nowrap';");
txtstream.WriteLine("}");
txtstream.WriteLine("span");
txtstream.WriteLine("{");
txtstream.WriteLine("    BORDER-RIGHT: #999999 3px solid;");
txtstream.WriteLine("    PADDING-RIGHT: 3px;");
txtstream.WriteLine("    PADDING-LEFT: 3px;");
txtstream.WriteLine("    FONT-WEIGHT: Normal;");
txtstream.WriteLine("    PADDING-BOTTOM: 3px;");
txtstream.WriteLine("    COLOR: white;");
txtstream.WriteLine("    PADDING-TOP: 3px;");
txtstream.WriteLine("    BORDER-BOTTOM: #999 1px solid;");
txtstream.WriteLine("    BACKGROUND-COLOR: navy;");
txtstream.WriteLine("    FONT-FAMILY: font-family: Cambria, serif;");
txtstream.WriteLine("    FONT-SIZE: 10px;");
txtstream.WriteLine("    text-align: left;");
txtstream.WriteLine("    white-Space: nowrap='nowrap';");
txtstream.WriteLine("    display: inline-block;");
txtstream.WriteLine("    width: 100%;");
txtstream.WriteLine("}");
txtstream.WriteLine("textarea");
txtstream.WriteLine("{");
txtstream.WriteLine("    BORDER-RIGHT: #999999 3px solid;");
txtstream.WriteLine("    PADDING-RIGHT: 3px;");
txtstream.WriteLine("    PADDING-LEFT: 3px;");
txtstream.WriteLine("    FONT-WEIGHT: Normal;");
txtstream.WriteLine("    PADDING-BOTTOM: 3px;");
txtstream.WriteLine("    COLOR: white;");
txtstream.WriteLine("    PADDING-TOP: 3px;");
txtstream.WriteLine("    BORDER-BOTTOM: #999 1px solid;");
txtstream.WriteLine("    BACKGROUND-COLOR: navy;");
txtstream.WriteLine("    FONT-FAMILY: font-family: Cambria, serif;");
txtstream.WriteLine("    FONT-SIZE: 10px;");
txtstream.WriteLine("    text-align: left;");
txtstream.WriteLine("    white-Space: nowrap='nowrap';");
txtstream.WriteLine("    width: 100%;");
txtstream.WriteLine("}");
txtstream.WriteLine("select");
txtstream.WriteLine("{");
txtstream.WriteLine("    BORDER-RIGHT: #999999 3px solid;");
txtstream.WriteLine("    PADDING-RIGHT: 6px;");
txtstream.WriteLine("    PADDING-LEFT: 6px;");
txtstream.WriteLine("    FONT-WEIGHT: Normal;");
txtstream.WriteLine("    PADDING-BOTTOM: 6px;");
txtstream.WriteLine("    COLOR: white;");
txtstream.WriteLine("    PADDING-TOP: 6px;");
txtstream.WriteLine("    BORDER-BOTTOM: #999 1px solid;");
txtstream.WriteLine("    BACKGROUND-COLOR: navy;");
```

```
txtstream.WriteLine("    FONT-FAMILY: font-family: Cambria, serif;");
txtstream.WriteLine("    FONT-SIZE: 10px;");
txtstream.WriteLine("    text-align: left;");
txtstream.WriteLine("    white-Space: nowrap='nowrap';");
txtstream.WriteLine("    width: 100%;");
txtstream.WriteLine("}");
txtstream.WriteLine("input");
txtstream.WriteLine("{");
txtstream.WriteLine("    BORDER-RIGHT: #999999 3px solid;");
txtstream.WriteLine("    PADDING-RIGHT: 3px;");
txtstream.WriteLine("    PADDING-LEFT: 3px;");
txtstream.WriteLine("    FONT-WEIGHT: Bold;");
txtstream.WriteLine("    PADDING-BOTTOM: 3px;");
txtstream.WriteLine("    COLOR: white;");
txtstream.WriteLine("    PADDING-TOP: 3px;");
txtstream.WriteLine("    BORDER-BOTTOM: #999 1px solid;");
txtstream.WriteLine("    BACKGROUND-COLOR: navy;");
txtstream.WriteLine("    FONT-FAMILY: font-family: Cambria, serif;");
txtstream.WriteLine("    FONT-SIZE: 12px;");
txtstream.WriteLine("    text-align: left;");
txtstream.WriteLine("    display: table-cell;");
txtstream.WriteLine("    white-Space: nowrap='nowrap';");
txtstream.WriteLine("    width: 100%;");
txtstream.WriteLine("}");
txtstream.WriteLine("h1 {");
txtstream.WriteLine("color: antiquewhite;");
txtstream.WriteLine("text-shadow: 1px 1px 1px black;");
txtstream.WriteLine("padding: 3px;");
txtstream.WriteLine("text-align: center;");
txtstream.WriteLine("box-shadow: inset 2px 2px 5px rgba(0,0,0,0.5), inset -2px -
2px 5px rgba(255,255,255,0.5);");
txtstream.WriteLine("}");
txtstream.WriteLine("</style>");
txtstream.WriteLine("<body>");
txtstream.WriteLine("<center>");
txtstream.WriteLine("</br>");
txtstream.WriteLine("</br>");
txtstream.WriteLine("<table border=0 cellspacing=3 cellpadding=3>");
txtstream.WriteLine("<tr>");
foreach col as System.Data.DataColumn in ds.Tables(0).Columns
{
    txtstream.WriteLine("<th align='left' nowrap='nowrap'>" + col.Caption +
"</th>");
}
txtstream.WriteLine("</tr>");

foreach row as System.Data.DataRow in ds.Tables(0).Rows
{
    txtstream.WriteLine("<tr>");
    foreach col as System.Data.DataColumn in ds.Tables(0).Columns
```

```
     {
          txtstream.WriteLine("<td  align='left' nowrap='true'><input type=text
value="""" + row[col.Caption].ToString() + """"></input></td>");
     }
     txtstream.WriteLine("</tr>");
}
txtstream.WriteLine("</table>");
txtstream.WriteLine("</body>");
txtstream.WriteLine("</html>");
txtstream.Close();
```

A LOT OF CODE TO COVER

Overview

THERE IS A LOT OF CODE TO COVER AND, HONESTLY, I HATE INTRODUCTIONS. So, let's make this short and sweet. We're using OLEDB and the Dataset to create outputs that include ASP, ASPX, Delimited Text Files, Excel, HTA, HTML, XML, and XSL. There, I said it, I'm done.

From the OLEDB Coding perspective, use the following:

```
string cnstr = "";
string strQuery = "";
```

Connection, Command and DataAdapter

```
System.Data.SQLClient.SQLConnection cn = new
System.Data.SQLClient.SQLConnection(cnstr);
cn.Open();

System.Data.SQLClient.SQLCommand cmd = new
System.Data.SQLClient.SQLCommand();
```

```
cmd.Connection = cn;"
cmd.CommandType = 1;
cmd.CommandText = strQuery;
cmd.ExecuteNonquery();

System.Data.SQLClient.SQLDataAdapter da = new
System.Data.SQLClient.SQLDataAdapter(cmd);
```

Connection and DataAdapter

```
System.Data.SQLClient.SQLConnection cn = new
System.Data.SQLClient.SQLConnection(cnstr);
cn.Open();

System.Data.SQLClient.SQLDataAdapter da = new
System.Data.SQLClient.SQLDataAdapter(strQuery, cn);
```

Command and DataAdapter

```
System.Data.SQLClient.SQLCommand cmd = new
System.Data.SQLClient.SQLCommand();
cmd.Connection = new System.Data.SQLClient.SQLConnection;"
cmd.Connection.ConnectionString = cnstr;")
cmd.Connection.Open();

cmd.CommandType = 1;
cmd.CommandText = strQuery;
cmd.ExecuteNonQuery();

System.Data.SQLClient.SQLDataAdapter da = new
System.Data.SQLClient.SQLDataAdapter(cmd);
```

DataAdapter

```
System.Data.SQLClient.SQLDataAdapter da = new
System.Data.SQLClient.SQLDataAdapter(strQuery, cnstr);
```

Dataset

```
System.Data.DataTable dt = new System.Data.DataSet;
da.Fill(dt);
```

You are going to need to add this to the routines to the code below because they and some additional code logic takes up way too many pages.

ASP EXAMPLES

Let's do it!

Below, are examples of using OLEDB, the Dataset and ASP. And just in case you are wondering, I use none as meaning no additional tags between the <td></td>

HORIZONTAL

```
Scripting.FileSystemObject fso = new Scripting.FileSystemObject();
Scripting.TextStream txtstream = fso.OpenTextFile(Application.StartupPath +
"\\Products.asp",IOMode.ForWriting, True, Tristate.TristateUseDefault);
txtstream.WriteLine("<html>");
txtstream.WriteLine("<head>");
txtstream.WriteLine("<title>Products</title>");
txtstream.WriteLine("<body>");
```

For Reports:

```
txtstream.WriteLine("<table border=0 cellspacing=3 cellpadding=3>");
```

For Tables:

```
txtstream.WriteLine("<table border=1 cellspacing=3 cellpadding=3>");

txtstream.WriteLine("<%");
txtstream.WriteLine("Response.Write(""<tr>"" & vbcrlf)");
foreach(System.Data.DataColumn col in dt.Columns)
{
```

```
        txtstream.WriteLine("Response.Write(""<th align='left' nowrap='nowrap'>" +
col.Caption + "</th>""" & vbcrlf)");
    }
    txtstream.WriteLine("Response.Write(""</tr>""" & vbcrlf)");
```

Additional Tags:

None

```
    foreach(System.Data.DataRow row in dt.Rows)
    {
        txtstream.WriteLine("Response.Write(""<tr>""" & vbcrlf)");
        foreach(System.Data.DataColumn col in dt.Columns)
        {
            txtstream.WriteLine("Response.Write(""<td align='left' nowrap='nowrap'>"
+ row[col.Caption].ToString() + "</td>""" & vbcrlf)");
        }
        txtstream.WriteLine("Response.Write(""</tr>""" & vbcrlf)");
    }
```

Button

```
    foreach(System.Data.DataRow row in dt.Rows)
    {
        txtstream.WriteLine("Response.Write(""<tr>""" & vbcrlf)");
        foreach(System.Data.DataColumn col in dt.Columns)
        {
            txtstream.WriteLine("Response.Write(""<td  align='left'
nowrap='true'><button style='width:100%;' value ='" + row[col.Caption].ToString()
+ "'>" + row[col.Caption].ToString() + "</button></td>""" & vbcrlf)");
        }
        txtstream.WriteLine("Response.Write(""</tr>""" & vbcrlf)");
    }
```

Combobox

```
    foreach(System.Data.DataRow row in dt.Rows)
    {
        txtstream.WriteLine("Response.Write(""<tr>""" & vbcrlf)");
        foreach(System.Data.DataColumn col in dt.Columns)
        {
            txtstream.WriteLine("Response.Write(""<td  align='left'
nowrap='true'><select><option value = """ + row[col.Caption].ToString() + """">" +
row[col.Caption].ToString() + "</option></select></td>""" & vbcrlf)");
        }
        txtstream.WriteLine("Response.Write(""</tr>""" & vbcrlf)");
    }
```

Div

```
foreach(System.Data.DataRow row in dt.Rows)
{
    txtstream.WriteLine("Response.Write(""<tr>"" & vbcrlf)");
    foreach(System.Data.DataColumn col in dt.Columns)
    {
        txtstream.WriteLine("Response.Write(""<td  align='left'
nowrap='true'><div>" + row[col.Caption].ToString() + "</div></td>"" & vbcrlf)");
    }
    txtstream.WriteLine("Response.Write(""</tr>"" & vbcrlf)");
}
```

Link

```
foreach(System.Data.DataRow row in dt.Rows)
{
    txtstream.WriteLine("Response.Write(""<tr>"" & vbcrlf)");
    foreach(System.Data.DataColumn col in dt.Columns)
    {
        txtstream.WriteLine("Response.Write(""<td align='left' nowrap='true'><a
href='" + row[col.Caption].ToString() + "'>" + row[col.Caption].ToString() +
"</a></td>"" & vbcrlf)");
    }
    txtstream.WriteLine("Response.Write(""</tr>"" & vbcrlf)");
}
```

Listbox

```
foreach(System.Data.DataRow row in dt.Rows)
{
    txtstream.WriteLine("Response.Write(""<tr>"" & vbcrlf)");
    foreach(System.Data.DataColumn col in dt.Columns)
    {
        txtstream.WriteLine("Response.Write(""<td  align='left'
nowrap='true'><select multiple><option value = """ + row[col.Caption].ToString() +
"""'>" + row[col.Caption].ToString() + "</option></select></td>"" & vbcrlf)");
    }
    txtstream.WriteLine("Response.Write(""</tr>"" & vbcrlf)");
}
```

Span

```
foreach(System.Data.DataRow row in dt.Rows)
{
```

```csharp
        txtstream.WriteLine("Response.Write(""<tr>"" & vbcrlf)");
        foreach(System.Data.DataColumn col in dt.Columns)
        {
            txtstream.WriteLine("Response.Write(""<td  align='left'
nowrap='true'><span>" + row[col.Caption].ToString() + "</span></td>"" &
vbcrlf)");
        }
        txtstream.WriteLine("Response.Write(""</tr>"" & vbcrlf)");
    }
```

Textarea

```csharp
    foreach(System.Data.DataRow row in dt.Rows)
    {
        txtstream.WriteLine("Response.Write(""<tr>"" & vbcrlf)");
        foreach(System.Data.DataColumn col in dt.Columns)
        {
            txtstream.WriteLine("Response.Write(""<td  align='left'
nowrap='true'><textarea>" + row[col.Caption].ToString() + "</textarea></td>"" &
vbcrlf)");
        }
        txtstream.WriteLine("Response.Write(""</tr>"" & vbcrlf)");
    }
```

Textbox

```csharp
    foreach(System.Data.DataRow row in dt.Rows)
    {
        txtstream.WriteLine("Response.Write(""<tr>"" & vbcrlf)");
        foreach(System.Data.DataColumn col in dt.Columns)
        {
            txtstream.WriteLine("Response.Write(""<td  align='left'
nowrap='true'><input type=text value=""""" + row[col.Caption].ToString() +
"""""></input></td>"" & vbcrlf)");
        }
        txtstream.WriteLine("Response.Write(""</tr>"" & vbcrlf)");
    }
```

End Code

```csharp
    txtstream.WriteLine("%>");
    txtstream.WriteLine("</table>");
    txtstream.WriteLine("</body>");
    txtstream.WriteLine("</html>");
    txtstream.Close();
```

VERTICAL

```
String cnstr ="" ;
string strQuery = "";

System.Data.SQLClient.SQLConnection cn = new
System.Data.SQLClient.SQLConnection(cnstr);
  cn.Open();

System.Data.SQLClient.SQLCommand cmd = new
System.Data.SQLClient.SQLCommand();
  cmd.Connection = cn;
  cmd.CommandType = 1;
  cmd.CommandText = strQuery;
  cmd.ExecuteNonquery();

System.Data.SQLClient.SQLDataAdapter da = new
System.Data.SQLClient.SQLDataAdapter(cmd);

System.Data.DataTable ds as new System.Data.Dataset();
da.Fill(dt);
Scripting.FileSystemObject fso = new Scripting.FileSystemObject();
Scripting.TextStream txtstream = fso.OpenTextFile(Application.StartupPath +
"\\Products.asp",IOMode.ForWriting, True, Tristate.TristateUseDefault);
  txtstream.WriteLine("<html>");
  txtstream.WriteLine("<head>");
  txtstream.WriteLine("<title>Products</title>");
  txtstream.WriteLine("<body>");
  txtstream.WriteLine("<center>");
  txtstream.WriteLine("</br>");
  txtstream.WriteLine("</br>");
```

For Reports:

```
  txtstream.WriteLine("<table border=0 cellspacing=3 cellpadding=3>");
```

For Tables:

```
  txtstream.WriteLine("<table border=1 cellspacing=3 cellpadding=3>");

  txtstream.WriteLine("<%");
  foreach(System.Data.DataColumn col in dt.Columns)
  {
    txtstream.WriteLine("Response.Write(""<tr><th align='left'
nowrap='nowrap'>" + col.Caption + "</th>""" & vbcrlf)");
```

```
foreach(System.Data.DataRow row in dt.Rows)
{
    txtstream.WriteLine("Response.Write(""<td  align='left' nowrap='nowrap'>"
+ row[col.Caption].ToString() + "</td>"" & vbcrlf)");
}
```

Additional Tags:

None

```
foreach(System.Data.DataRow row in dt.Rows)
{
    txtstream.WriteLine("Response.Write(""<td  align='left' nowrap='nowrap'>"
+ row[col.Caption].ToString() + "</td>"" & vbcrlf)");
}
```

Button

```
foreach(System.Data.DataRow row in dt.Rows)
{
    txtstream.WriteLine("Response.Write(""<td  align='left'
nowrap='true'><button style='width:100%;' value ='" + row[col.Caption].ToString()
+ "'>" + row[col.Caption].ToString() + "</button></td>"" & vbcrlf)");
}
```

Combobox

```
foreach(System.Data.DataRow row in dt.Rows)
{
    txtstream.WriteLine("Response.Write(""<td  align='left'
nowrap='true'><select><option value = """ + row[col.Caption].ToString() + """>" +
row[col.Caption].ToString() + "</option></select></td>"" & vbcrlf)");
}
```

Div

```
foreach(System.Data.DataRow row in dt.Rows)
{
    txtstream.WriteLine("Response.Write(""<td  align='left'
nowrap='true'><div>" + row[col.Caption].ToString() + "</div></td>"" & vbcrlf)");
}
```

Link

```
foreach(System.Data.DataRow row in dt.Rows)
{
    txtstream.WriteLine("Response.Write(""<td  align='left' nowrap='true'><a
href='" + row[col.Caption].ToString() + "'>" + row[col.Caption].ToString() +
"</a></td>"" & vbcrlf)");
}
```

Listbox

```
foreach(System.Data.DataRow row in dt.Rows)
{
    txtstream.WriteLine("Response.Write(""<td  align='left'
nowrap='true'><select multiple><option value = """ + row[col.Caption].ToString() +
""">" + row[col.Caption].ToString() + "</option></select></td>"" & vbcrlf)");
}
```

Span

```
foreach(System.Data.DataRow row in dt.Rows)
{
    txtstream.WriteLine("Response.Write(""<td  align='left'
nowrap='true'><span>" + row[col.Caption].ToString() + "</span></td>"" &
vbcrlf)");
}
```

Textarea

```
foreach(System.Data.DataRow row in dt.Rows)
{
    txtstream.WriteLine("Response.Write(""<td  align='left'
nowrap='true'><textarea>" + row[col.Caption].ToString() + "</textarea></td>"" &
vbcrlf)");
}
```

Textbox

```
foreach(System.Data.DataRow row in dt.Rows)
{
    txtstream.WriteLine("Response.Write(""<td  align='left'
nowrap='true'><input type=text value=""" + row[col.Caption].ToString() +
""></input></td>"" & vbcrlf)");
}
```

```
    txtstream.WriteLine("Response.Write(""</tr>"" & vbcrlf)");
}
txtstream.WriteLine("%>");
txtstream.WriteLine("</table>");
txtstream.WriteLine("</body>");
txtstream.WriteLine("</html>");
txtstream.Close();
```

ASPX EXAMPLES

Yes you can!

B elow, are examples of using OLEDB, the Dataset and ASP. And just in case you are wondering, I use none as meaning no additional tags between the <td></td>

HORIZONTAL

```
Scripting.FileSystemObject fso = new Scripting.FileSystemObject();
Scripting.TextStream txtstream = fso.OpenTextFile(Application.StartupPath +
"\\Products.asp",IOMode.ForWriting, True, Tristate.TristateUseDefault);
txtstream.WriteLine("<html>");
txtstream.WriteLine("<head>");
txtstream.WriteLine("<title>Products</title>");
txtstream.WriteLine("<body>");
```

For Reports:

```
txtstream.WriteLine("<table border=0 cellspacing=3 cellpadding=3>");
```

For Tables:

```
txtstream.WriteLine("<table border=1 cellspacing=3 cellpadding=3>");

txtstream.WriteLine("<%");
```

```
txtstream.WriteLine("Response.Write(""<tr>"" & vbcrlf)");
foreach(System.Data.DataColumn col in dt.Columns)
{
    txtstream.WriteLine("Response.Write(""<th align='left' nowrap='nowrap'>" +
col.Caption + "</th>"" & vbcrlf)");
}
txtstream.WriteLine("Response.Write(""</tr>"" & vbcrlf)");
```

Additional Tags:

None

```
foreach(System.Data.DataRow row in dt.Rows)
{
    txtstream.WriteLine("Response.Write(""<tr>"" & vbcrlf)");
    foreach(System.Data.DataColumn col in dt.Columns)
    {
        txtstream.WriteLine("Response.Write(""<td align='left' nowrap='nowrap'>"
+ row[col.Caption].ToString() + "</td>"" & vbcrlf)");
    }
    txtstream.WriteLine("Response.Write(""</tr>"" & vbcrlf)");
}
```

Button

```
foreach(System.Data.DataRow row in dt.Rows)
{
    txtstream.WriteLine("Response.Write(""<tr>"" & vbcrlf)");
    foreach(System.Data.DataColumn col in dt.Columns)
    {
        txtstream.WriteLine("Response.Write(""<td align='left'
nowrap='true'><button style='width:100%;' value ='" + row[col.Caption].ToString()
+ "'>" + row[col.Caption].ToString() + "</button></td>"" & vbcrlf)");
    }
    txtstream.WriteLine("Response.Write(""</tr>"" & vbcrlf)");
}
```

Combobox

```
foreach(System.Data.DataRow row in dt.Rows)
{
    txtstream.WriteLine("Response.Write(""<tr>"" & vbcrlf)");
    foreach(System.Data.DataColumn col in dt.Columns)
    {
        txtstream.WriteLine("Response.Write(""<td align='left'
nowrap='true'><select><option value = """ + row[col.Caption].ToString() + """>" +
row[col.Caption].ToString() + "</option></select></td>"" & vbcrlf)");
```

```
        }
        txtstream.WriteLine("Response.Write(""</tr>""" & vbcrlf)");
    }
```

Div

```
    foreach(System.Data.DataRow row in dt.Rows)
    {
        txtstream.WriteLine("Response.Write(""<tr>""" & vbcrlf)");
        foreach(System.Data.DataColumn col in dt.Columns)
        {
            txtstream.WriteLine("Response.Write(""<td  align='left'
nowrap='true'><div>" + row[col.Caption].ToString() + "</div></td>""" & vbcrlf)");
        }
        txtstream.WriteLine("Response.Write(""</tr>""" & vbcrlf)");
    }
```

Link

```
    foreach(System.Data.DataRow row in dt.Rows)
    {
        txtstream.WriteLine("Response.Write(""<tr>""" & vbcrlf)");
        foreach(System.Data.DataColumn col in dt.Columns)
        {
            txtstream.WriteLine("Response.Write(""<td  align='left' nowrap='true'><a
href='" + row[col.Caption].ToString() + "'>" + row[col.Caption].ToString() +
"</a></td>""" & vbcrlf)");
        }
        txtstream.WriteLine("Response.Write(""</tr>""" & vbcrlf)");
    }
```

Listbox

```
    foreach(System.Data.DataRow row in dt.Rows)
    {
        txtstream.WriteLine("Response.Write(""<tr>""" & vbcrlf)");
        foreach(System.Data.DataColumn col in dt.Columns)
        {
            txtstream.WriteLine("Response.Write(""<td  align='left'
nowrap='true'><select multiple><option value = """ + row[col.Caption].ToString() +
"""">" + row[col.Caption].ToString() + "</option></select></td>""" & vbcrlf)");
        }
        txtstream.WriteLine("Response.Write(""</tr>""" & vbcrlf)");
    }
```

```
foreach(System.Data.DataRow row in dt.Rows)
{
    txtstream.WriteLine("Response.Write(""<tr>"" & vbcrlf)");
    foreach(System.Data.DataColumn col in dt.Columns)
    {
        txtstream.WriteLine("Response.Write(""<td align='left'
nowrap='true'><span>" + row[col.Caption].ToString() + "</span></td>"" &
vbcrlf)");
    }
    txtstream.WriteLine("Response.Write(""</tr>"" & vbcrlf)");
}
```

Textarea

```
foreach(System.Data.DataRow row in dt.Rows)
{
    txtstream.WriteLine("Response.Write(""<tr>"" & vbcrlf)");
    foreach(System.Data.DataColumn col in dt.Columns)
    {
        txtstream.WriteLine("Response.Write(""<td align='left'
nowrap='true'><textarea>" + row[col.Caption].ToString() + "</textarea></td>"" &
vbcrlf)");
    }
    txtstream.WriteLine("Response.Write(""</tr>"" & vbcrlf)");
}
```
Textbox

```
foreach(System.Data.DataRow row in dt.Rows)
{
    txtstream.WriteLine("Response.Write(""<tr>"" & vbcrlf)");
    foreach(System.Data.DataColumn col in dt.Columns)
    {
        txtstream.WriteLine("Response.Write(""<td align='left'
nowrap='true'><input type=text value=""" + row[col.Caption].ToString() +
"""></input></td>"" & vbcrlf)");
    }
    txtstream.WriteLine("Response.Write(""</tr>"" & vbcrlf)");
}
```

End Code

```
txtstream.WriteLine("%>");
txtstream.WriteLine("</table>");
txtstream.WriteLine("</body>");
txtstream.WriteLine("</html>");
```

```
txtstream.Close();
```


VERTICAL


```
Scripting.FileSystemObject fso = new Scripting.FileSystemObject();
Scripting.TextStream txtstream = fso.OpenTextFile(Application.StartupPath +
"\\Products.asp",IOMode.ForWriting, True, Tristate.TristateUseDefault);
txtstream.WriteLine("<html>");
txtstream.WriteLine("<head>");
txtstream.WriteLine("<title>Products</title>");
txtstream.WriteLine("<body>");
txtstream.WriteLine("<center>");
txtstream.WriteLine("</br>");
txtstream.WriteLine("</br>");
```

For Reports:

```
txtstream.WriteLine("<table border=0 cellspacing=3 cellpadding=3>");
```

For Tables:

```
txtstream.WriteLine("<table border=1 cellspacing=3 cellpadding=3>");

txtstream.WriteLine("<%");
foreach(System.Data.DataColumn col in dt.Columns)
{
    txtstream.WriteLine("Response.Write(""<tr><th align='left'
nowrap='nowrap'>" + col.Caption + "</th>""" & vbcrlf)");
```


None


```
foreach(System.Data.DataRow row in dt.Rows)
{
    txtstream.WriteLine("Response.Write(""<td  align='left' nowrap='nowrap'>"
+ row[col.Caption].ToString() + "</td>""" & vbcrlf)");
}
```

Additional Tags:

```
foreach(System.Data.DataRow row in dt.Rows)
{
    txtstream.WriteLine("Response.Write(""<td align='left' nowrap='nowrap'>"
+ row[col.Caption].ToString() + "</td>"" & vbcrlf)");
}
```

```
foreach(System.Data.DataRow row in dt.Rows)
{
    txtstream.WriteLine("Response.Write(""<td align='left'
nowrap='true'><button style='width:100%;' value ='" + row[col.Caption].ToString()
+ "'>" + row[col.Caption].ToString() + "</button></td>"" & vbcrlf)");
}
```

```
foreach(System.Data.DataRow row in dt.Rows)
{
    txtstream.WriteLine("Response.Write(""<td align='left'
nowrap='true'><select><option value = """ + row[col.Caption].ToString() + """>" +
row[col.Caption].ToString() + "</option></select></td>"" & vbcrlf)");
}
```

```
foreach(System.Data.DataRow row in dt.Rows)
{
    txtstream.WriteLine("Response.Write(""<td align='left'
nowrap='true'><div>" + row[col.Caption].ToString() + "</div></td>"" & vbcrlf)");
}
```

```
foreach(System.Data.DataRow row in dt.Rows)
{
    txtstream.WriteLine("Response.Write(""<td align='left' nowrap='true'><a
href='" + row[col.Caption].ToString() + "'>" + row[col.Caption].ToString() +
"</a></td>"" & vbcrlf)");
}
```

```
foreach(System.Data.DataRow row in dt.Rows)
{
    txtstream.WriteLine("Response.Write(""<td  align='left'
nowrap='true'><select multiple><option value = """ + row[col.Caption].ToString() +
""">" + row[col.Caption].ToString() + "</option></select></td>"" & vbcrlf)");
}
```

```
foreach(System.Data.DataRow row in dt.Rows)
{
    txtstream.WriteLine("Response.Write(""<td  align='left'
nowrap='true'><span>" + row[col.Caption].ToString() + "</span></td>"" &
vbcrlf)");
}
```

```
foreach(System.Data.DataRow row in dt.Rows)
{
    txtstream.WriteLine("Response.Write(""<td  align='left'
nowrap='true'><textarea>" + row[col.Caption].ToString() + "</textarea></td>"" &
vbcrlf)");
}
```

```
foreach(System.Data.DataRow row in dt.Rows)
{
    txtstream.WriteLine("Response.Write(""<td  align='left'
nowrap='true'><input type=text value=""" + row[col.Caption].ToString() +
"""></input></td>"" & vbcrlf)");
}
```

```
    txtstream.WriteLine("Response.Write(""</tr>"" & vbcrlf)");
}
txtstream.WriteLine("%>");
txtstream.WriteLine("</table>");
txtstream.WriteLine("</body>");
txtstream.WriteLine("</html>");
txtstream.Close();
```

HTA EXAMPLES

Let's do it!

B elow, are examples of using OLEDB, the Dataset and ASP. And just in case you are wondering, I use none as meaning no additional tags between the <td></td>

HORIZONTAL

```
Scripting.FileSystemObject fso = new Scripting.FileSystemObject();
Scripting.TextStream txtstream = fso.OpenTextFile(Application.StartupPath +
"\\Products.asp",IOMode.ForWriting, True, Tristate.TristateUseDefault);
txtstream.WriteLine("<html>");
txtstream.WriteLine("<head>");
txtstream.WriteLine("<HTA:APPLICATION ");
txtstream.WriteLine("ID = 'Products' ");
txtstream.WriteLine("APPLICATIONNAME = 'Products' ");
txtstream.WriteLine("SCROLL = 'yes' ");
txtstream.WriteLine("SINGLEINSTANCE = 'yes' ");
txtstream.WriteLine("WINDOWSTATE = 'maximize' >");
txtstream.WriteLine("<title>Products</title>");
txtstream.WriteLine("<body>");
```

For Reports:

```
txtstream.WriteLine("<table border=0 cellspacing=3 cellpadding=3>");
```

For Tables:

```
txtstream.WriteLine("<table border=1 cellspacing=3 cellpadding=3>");

txtstream.WriteLine("<%");
txtstream.WriteLine("<tr>");
foreach(System.Data.DataColumn col in dt.Columns)
{
    txtstream.WriteLine("<th align='left' nowrap='nowrap'>" +   col.Caption +
"</th>");
}
txtstream.WriteLine("</tr>");
```

Additional Tags:

None

```
foreach(System.Data.DataRow row in dt.Rows)
{
    txtstream.WriteLine("<tr>");
    foreach(System.Data.DataColumn col in dt.Columns)
    {
        txtstream.WriteLine("<td  align='left' nowrap='nowrap'>" +
row[col.Caption].ToString() + "</td>");
    }
    txtstream.WriteLine("</tr>");
}
```

Button

```
foreach(System.Data.DataRow row in dt.Rows)
{
    txtstream.WriteLine("<tr>");
    foreach(System.Data.DataColumn col in dt.Columns)
    {
        txtstream.WriteLine("<td  align='left' nowrap='true'><button
style='width:100%;' value ='" + row[col.Caption].ToString() + "'>" +
row[col.Caption].ToString() + "</button></td>");
    }
    txtstream.WriteLine("</tr>");
}
```

Combobox

```
foreach(System.Data.DataRow row in dt.Rows)
{
```

```csharp
        txtstream.WriteLine("<tr>");
        foreach(System.Data.DataColumn col in dt.Columns)
        {
            txtstream.WriteLine("<td  align='left' nowrap='true'><select><option value
= '"'" + row[col.Caption].ToString() + "'"'>" + row[col.Caption].ToString() +
"</option></select></td>");
        }
        txtstream.WriteLine("</tr>");
    }
```

Div

```csharp
    foreach(System.Data.DataRow row in dt.Rows)
    {
        txtstream.WriteLine("<tr>");
        foreach(System.Data.DataColumn col in dt.Columns)
        {
            txtstream.WriteLine("<td  align='left' nowrap='true'><div>" +
row[col.Caption].ToString() + "</div></td>");
        }
        txtstream.WriteLine("</tr>");
    }
```

Link

```csharp
    foreach(System.Data.DataRow row in dt.Rows)
    {
        txtstream.WriteLine("<tr>");
        foreach(System.Data.DataColumn col in dt.Columns)
        {
            txtstream.WriteLine("<td  align='left' nowrap='true'><a href='" +
row[col.Caption].ToString() + "'>" + row[col.Caption].ToString() + "</a></td>");
        }
        txtstream.WriteLine("</tr>");
    }
```

Listbox

```csharp
    foreach(System.Data.DataRow row in dt.Rows)
    {
        txtstream.WriteLine("<tr>");
        foreach(System.Data.DataColumn col in dt.Columns)
        {
            txtstream.WriteLine("<td  align='left' nowrap='true'><select
multiple><option value = '"'" + row[col.Caption].ToString() + "'"'>" +
row[col.Caption].ToString() + "</option></select></td>");
        }
```

```csharp
        txtstream.WriteLine("</tr>");
    }
```

```csharp
    foreach(System.Data.DataRow row in dt.Rows)
    {
        txtstream.WriteLine("<tr>");
        foreach(System.Data.DataColumn col in dt.Columns)
        {
            txtstream.WriteLine("<td  align='left' nowrap='true'><span>" +
row[col.Caption].ToString() + "</span></td>");
        }
        txtstream.WriteLine("</tr>");
    }
```

```csharp
    foreach(System.Data.DataRow row in dt.Rows)
    {
        txtstream.WriteLine("<tr>");
        foreach(System.Data.DataColumn col in dt.Columns)
        {
            txtstream.WriteLine("<td  align='left' nowrap='true'><textarea>" +
row[col.Caption].ToString() + "</textarea></td>");
        }
        txtstream.WriteLine("</tr>");
    }
```

```csharp
    foreach(System.Data.DataRow row in dt.Rows)
    {
        txtstream.WriteLine("<tr>");
        foreach(System.Data.DataColumn col in dt.Columns)
        {
            txtstream.WriteLine("<td  align='left' nowrap='true'><input type=text
value="""" + row[col.Caption].ToString() + """"></input></td>");
        }
        txtstream.WriteLine("</tr>");
    }
```

```csharp
    txtstream.WriteLine("%>");
    txtstream.WriteLine("</table>");
    txtstream.WriteLine("</body>");
```

```
txtstream.WriteLine("</html>");
txtstream.Close();
```

VERTICAL

```
string cnstr = "";
string strQuery = "";

System.Data.SQLClient.SQLConnection cn = new
System.Data.SQLClient.SQLConnection(cnstr);
cn.Open();

System.Data.SQLClient.SQLCommand cmd = new
System.Data.SQLClient.SQLCommand();
cmd.Connection = cn;
cmd.CommandType = 1;
cmd.CommandText = strQuery;
cmd.ExecuteNonquery();

System.Data.SQLClient.SQLDataAdapter da = new
System.Data.SQLClient.SQLDataAdapter(cmd);

System.Data.DataTable ds as new System.Data.Dataset();
da.Fill(dt);
Scripting.FileSystemObject fso = new Scripting.FileSystemObject();
Scripting.TextStream txtstream = fso.OpenTextFile(Application.StartupPath +
"\\Products.asp",IOMode.ForWriting, True, Tristate.TristateUseDefault);
txtstream.WriteLine("<html>");
txtstream.WriteLine("<head>");
txtstream.WriteLine("<title>Products</title>");
txtstream.WriteLine("<body>");
txtstream.WriteLine("<center>");
txtstream.WriteLine("</br>");
txtstream.WriteLine("</br>");
```

For Reports:

```
txtstream.WriteLine("<table border=0 cellspacing=3 cellpadding=3>");
```

For Tables:

```
txtstream.WriteLine("<table border=1 cellspacing=3 cellpadding=3>");

txtstream.WriteLine("<%");
foreach(System.Data.DataColumn col in dt.Columns)
{
```

```
txtstream.WriteLine("<tr><th align='left' nowrap='nowrap'>" + col.Caption +
"</th>");
```

None

```
foreach(System.Data.DataRow row in dt.Rows)
{
    txtstream.WriteLine("<td align='left' nowrap='nowrap'>" +
row[col.Caption].ToString() + "</td>");
}
```

Additional Tags:

None

```
foreach(System.Data.DataRow row in dt.Rows)
{
    txtstream.WriteLine("<td align='left' nowrap='nowrap'>" +
row[col.Caption].ToString() + "</td>");
}
```

Button

```
foreach(System.Data.DataRow row in dt.Rows)
{
    txtstream.WriteLine("<td align='left' nowrap='true'><button
style='width:100%;' value ='" + row[col.Caption].ToString() + "'>" +
row[col.Caption].ToString() + "</button></td>");
}
```

Combobox

```
foreach(System.Data.DataRow row in dt.Rows)
{
    txtstream.WriteLine("<td align='left' nowrap='true'><select><option value
= """ + row[col.Caption].ToString() + """>" + row[col.Caption].ToString() +
"</option></select></td>");
}
```

Div

```
foreach(System.Data.DataRow row in dt.Rows)
```

```
    {
        txtstream.WriteLine("<td align='left' nowrap='true'><div>" +
row[col.Caption].ToString() + "</div></td>");
    }
```

Link

```
    foreach(System.Data.DataRow row in dt.Rows)
    {
        txtstream.WriteLine("<td align='left' nowrap='true'><a href='" +
row[col.Caption].ToString() + "'>" + row[col.Caption].ToString() + "</a></td>");
    }
```

Listbox

```
    foreach(System.Data.DataRow row in dt.Rows)
    {
        txtstream.WriteLine("<td align='left' nowrap='true'><select
multiple><option value = """ + row[col.Caption].ToString() + """>" +
row[col.Caption].ToString() + "</option></select></td>");
    }
```

Span

```
    foreach(System.Data.DataRow row in dt.Rows)
    {
        txtstream.WriteLine("<td align='left' nowrap='true'><span>" +
row[col.Caption].ToString() + "</span></td>");
    }
```

Textarea

```
    foreach(System.Data.DataRow row in dt.Rows)
    {
        txtstream.WriteLine("<td align='left' nowrap='true'><textarea>" +
row[col.Caption].ToString() + "</textarea></td>");
    }
```

Textbox

```
    foreach(System.Data.DataRow row in dt.Rows)
    {
        txtstream.WriteLine("<td align='left' nowrap='true'><input type=text
value=""" + row[col.Caption].ToString() + """></input></td>");
    }
```

```
    txtstream.WriteLine("</tr>");
}
txtstream.WriteLine("%>");
txtstream.WriteLine("</table>");
txtstream.WriteLine("</body>");
txtstream.WriteLine("</html>");
txtstream.Close();
```

HTA EXAMPLES

Let's do it!

B elow, are examples of using OLEDB, the Dataset and ASP. And just in case you are wondering, I use none as meaning no additional tags between the <td></td>

HORIZONTAL

```
Scripting.FileSystemObject fso = new Scripting.FileSystemObject();
Scripting.TextStream txtstream = fso.OpenTextFile(Application.StartupPath +
"\\Products.asp",IOMode.ForWriting, True, Tristate.TristateUseDefault);
txtstream.WriteLine("<html>");
txtstream.WriteLine("<head>");
txtstream.WriteLine("<title>Products</title>");
txtstream.WriteLine("<body>");
```

For Reports:

```
txtstream.WriteLine("<table border=0 cellspacing=3 cellpadding=3>");
```

For Tables:

```
txtstream.WriteLine("<table border=1 cellspacing=3 cellpadding=3>");
```

```
txtstream.WriteLine("<%");
txtstream.WriteLine("<tr>");
foreach(System.Data.DataColumn col in dt.Columns)
{
    txtstream.WriteLine("<th align='left' nowrap='nowrap'>" +    col.Caption +
"</th>");
}
txtstream.WriteLine("</tr>");
```

Additional Tags:

None

```
foreach(System.Data.DataRow row in dt.Rows)
{
    txtstream.WriteLine("<tr>");
    foreach(System.Data.DataColumn col in dt.Columns)
    {
        txtstream.WriteLine("<td  align='left' nowrap='nowrap'>" +
row[col.Caption].ToString() + "</td>");
    }
    txtstream.WriteLine("</tr>");
}
```

Button

```
foreach(System.Data.DataRow row in dt.Rows)
{
    txtstream.WriteLine("<tr>");
    foreach(System.Data.DataColumn col in dt.Columns)
    {
        txtstream.WriteLine("<td  align='left' nowrap='true'><button
style='width:100%;' value ='" + row[col.Caption].ToString() + "'>" +
row[col.Caption].ToString() + "</button></td>");
    }
    txtstream.WriteLine("</tr>");
}
```

Combobox

```
foreach(System.Data.DataRow row in dt.Rows)
{
    txtstream.WriteLine("<tr>");
    foreach(System.Data.DataColumn col in dt.Columns)
    {
```

```
        txtstream.WriteLine("<td align='left' nowrap='true'><select><option value
= "'" + row[col.Caption].ToString() + "'">" + row[col.Caption].ToString() +
"</option></select></td>");
    }
    txtstream.WriteLine("</tr>");
}
```

Div

```
foreach(System.Data.DataRow row in dt.Rows)
{
    txtstream.WriteLine("<tr>");
    foreach(System.Data.DataColumn col in dt.Columns)
    {
        txtstream.WriteLine("<td align='left' nowrap='true'><div>" +
row[col.Caption].ToString() + "</div></td>");
    }
    txtstream.WriteLine("</tr>");
}
```

Link

```
foreach(System.Data.DataRow row in dt.Rows)
{
    txtstream.WriteLine("<tr>");
    foreach(System.Data.DataColumn col in dt.Columns)
    {
        txtstream.WriteLine("<td align='left' nowrap='true'><a href='" +
row[col.Caption].ToString() + "'>" + row[col.Caption].ToString() + "</a></td>");
    }
    txtstream.WriteLine("</tr>");
}
```

Listbox

```
foreach(System.Data.DataRow row in dt.Rows)
{
    txtstream.WriteLine("<tr>");
    foreach(System.Data.DataColumn col in dt.Columns)
    {
        txtstream.WriteLine("<td align='left' nowrap='true'><select
multiple><option value = "'" + row[col.Caption].ToString() + "'">" +
row[col.Caption].ToString() + "</option></select></td>");
    }
    txtstream.WriteLine("</tr>");
}
```

```
foreach(System.Data.DataRow row in dt.Rows)
{
    txtstream.WriteLine("<tr>");
    foreach(System.Data.DataColumn col in dt.Columns)
    {
        txtstream.WriteLine("<td  align='left' nowrap='true'><span>" +
row[col.Caption].ToString() + "</span></td>");
    }
    txtstream.WriteLine("</tr>");
}
```

Textarea

```
foreach(System.Data.DataRow row in dt.Rows)
{
    txtstream.WriteLine("<tr>");
    foreach(System.Data.DataColumn col in dt.Columns)
    {
        txtstream.WriteLine("<td  align='left' nowrap='true'><textarea>" +
row[col.Caption].ToString() + "</textarea></td>");
    }
    txtstream.WriteLine("</tr>");
}
```

Textbox

```
foreach(System.Data.DataRow row in dt.Rows)
{
    txtstream.WriteLine("<tr>");
    foreach(System.Data.DataColumn col in dt.Columns)
    {
        txtstream.WriteLine("<td  align='left' nowrap='true'><input type=text
value='""" + row[col.Caption].ToString() + """'></input></td>");
    }
    txtstream.WriteLine("</tr>");
}
```

End Code

```
txtstream.WriteLine("%>");
txtstream.WriteLine("</table>");
txtstream.WriteLine("</body>");
txtstream.WriteLine("</html>");
txtstream.Close();
```

VERTICAL

```
string cnstr = "";
string strQuery = "";

System.Data.SQLClient.SQLConnection cn = new
System.Data.SQLClient.SQLConnection(cnstr);
cn.Open();

System.Data.SQLClient.SQLCommand cmd = new
System.Data.SQLClient.SQLCommand();
cmd.Connection = cn;
cmd.CommandType = 1;
cmd.CommandText = strQuery;
cmd.ExecuteNonquery();

System.Data.SQLClient.SQLDataAdapter da = new
System.Data.SQLClient.SQLDataAdapter(cmd);

System.Data.DataTable ds as new System.Data.Dataset();
da.Fill(dt);
Scripting.FileSystemObject fso = new Scripting.FileSystemObject();
Scripting.TextStream txtstream = fso.OpenTextFile(Application.StartupPath +
"\\Products.asp",IOMode.ForWriting, True, Tristate.TristateUseDefault);
txtstream.WriteLine("<html>");
txtstream.WriteLine("<head>");
txtstream.WriteLine("<title>Products</title>");
txtstream.WriteLine("<body>");
txtstream.WriteLine("<center>");
txtstream.WriteLine("</br>");
txtstream.WriteLine("</br>");
```

For Reports:

```
txtstream.WriteLine("<table border=0 cellspacing=3 cellpadding=3>");
```

For Tables:

```
txtstream.WriteLine("<table border=1 cellspacing=3 cellpadding=3>");

txtstream.WriteLine("<%");
foreach(System.Data.DataColumn col in dt.Columns)
{
    txtstream.WriteLine("<tr><th align='left' nowrap='nowrap'>" + col.Caption +
"</th>");
```

```
foreach(System.Data.DataRow row in dt.Rows)
{
    txtstream.WriteLine("<td  align='left' nowrap='nowrap'>" +
row[col.Caption].ToString() + "</td>");
}
```

Additional Tags:

None

```
foreach(System.Data.DataRow row in dt.Rows)
{
    txtstream.WriteLine("<td  align='left' nowrap='nowrap'>" +
row[col.Caption].ToString() + "</td>");
}
```

Button

```
foreach(System.Data.DataRow row in dt.Rows)
{
    txtstream.WriteLine("<td  align='left' nowrap='true'><button
style='width:100%;' value ='" + row[col.Caption].ToString() + "'>" +
row[col.Caption].ToString() + "</button></td>");
}
```

Combobox

```
foreach(System.Data.DataRow row in dt.Rows)
{
    txtstream.WriteLine("<td  align='left' nowrap='true'><select><option value
= '''" + row[col.Caption].ToString() + "'''>" + row[col.Caption].ToString() +
"</option></select></td>");
}
```

Div

```
foreach(System.Data.DataRow row in dt.Rows)
{
    txtstream.WriteLine("<td  align='left' nowrap='true'><div>" +
row[col.Caption].ToString() + "</div></td>");
}
```

```
        foreach(System.Data.DataRow row in dt.Rows)
        {
            txtstream.WriteLine("<td  align='left' nowrap='true'><a href='" +
row[col.Caption].ToString() + "'>" + row[col.Caption].ToString() + "</a></td>");
        }
```

Listbox

```
        foreach(System.Data.DataRow row in dt.Rows)
        {
            txtstream.WriteLine("<td  align='left' nowrap='true'><select
multiple><option value = "'" + row[col.Caption].ToString() + "'">" +
row[col.Caption].ToString() + "</option></select></td>");
        }
```

Span

```
        foreach(System.Data.DataRow row in dt.Rows)
        {
            txtstream.WriteLine("<td  align='left' nowrap='true'><span>" +
row[col.Caption].ToString() + "</span></td>");
        }
```

Textarea

```
        foreach(System.Data.DataRow row in dt.Rows)
        {
            txtstream.WriteLine("<td  align='left' nowrap='true'><textarea>" +
row[col.Caption].ToString() + "</textarea></td>");
        }
```

Textbox

```
        foreach(System.Data.DataRow row in dt.Rows)
        {
            txtstream.WriteLine("<td  align='left' nowrap='true'><input type=text
value="'" + row[col.Caption].ToString() + "'"></input></td>");
        }
```

End Code

```
        txtstream.WriteLine("</tr>");
```

```
}
txtstream.WriteLine("%>");
txtstream.WriteLine("</table>");
txtstream.WriteLine("</body>");
txtstream.WriteLine("</html>");
txtstream.Close();
```

DELIMITED TEXT FILES

BELOW ARE THE POPULAR EXAMPLES OF DIFFERENT DELIMITED TEXT FILES.

COLON DELIMITED HORIZONTAL VIEW

```
String tempstr = "";

Scripting.FileSystemObject fso = new Scripting.FileSystemObject();
Scripting.TextStream txtstream = fso.OpenTextFile(Application.StartupPath +
"\Products.txt",IOMode.ForWriting, True, Tristate.TristateUseDefault);
foreach(System.Data.DataColumn col in dt.Columns)
{
   if (tempstr != "")
   {
      tempstr = tempstr + ":";
   }
   tempstr = tempstr + col.Caption;
}
txtstream.WriteLine(tempstr);
tempstr = "";

foreach(System.Data.DataRow row in dt.Rows)
{
   foreach(System.Data.DataColumn col in dt.Columns)
   {
      if (tempstr != "")
      {
         tempstr = tempstr + ":";
```

```
        }
        tempstr = tempstr + (char)34 + row[col.Caption].ToString() + (char)34;
    }
    txtstream.WriteLine(tempstr);
    tempstr = "";

}
txtstream.Close();
```

COLON DELIMITED VERTICAL VIEW

```
String tempstr = "";


Scripting.FileSystemObject fso = new Scripting.FileSystemObject();
Scripting.TextStream txtstream = fso.OpenTextFile(Application.StartupPath +
"\Products.txt",IOMode.ForWriting, True, Tristate.TristateUseDefault);
foreach(System.Data.DataColumn col in dt.Columns)
{
    tempstr = col.Caption;
    foreach(System.Data.DataRow row in dt.Rows)
    {
        if (tempstr != "")
        {
            tempstr = tempstr + ":";
        }
            tempstr = tempstr + (char)34 + row[col.Caption].ToString() + (char)34;
    }
    txtstream.WriteLine(tempstr);
    tempstr = "";

}
txtstream.Close();
```

COMMA DELIMITED HORIZONTAL VIEW

```
String tempstr = "";


Scripting.FileSystemObject fso = new Scripting.FileSystemObject();
Scripting.TextStream txtstream = fso.OpenTextFile(Application.StartupPath +
"\Products.csv",IOMode.ForWriting, True, Tristate.TristateUseDefault);
foreach(System.Data.DataColumn col in dt.Columns)
{
    if (tempstr != "")
    {
```

```
        tempstr = tempstr + ",";
    }
    tempstr = tempstr + col.Caption;
}
txtstream.WriteLine(tempstr);
tempstr = "";

foreach(System.Data.DataRow row in dt.Rows)
{
    foreach(System.Data.DataColumn col in dt.Columns)
    {
        if (tempstr != "")
        {
            tempstr = tempstr + ",";
        }
            tempstr = tempstr + (char)34 + row[col.Caption].ToString() + (char)34;
        }
        txtstream.WriteLine(tempstr);
        tempstr = "";

}
txtstream.Close();
```

COMMA DELIMITED VERTICAL VIEW

```
String tempstr = "";

Scripting.FileSystemObject fso = new Scripting.FileSystemObject();
Scripting.TextStream txtstream = fso.OpenTextFile(Application.StartupPath +
"\Products.csv",IOMode.ForWriting, True, Tristate.TristateUseDefault);
foreach(System.Data.DataColumn col in dt.Columns)
{
    tempstr = col.Caption;
    foreach(System.Data.DataRow row in dt.Rows)
    {
        if (tempstr != "")
        {
            tempstr = tempstr + ",";
        }
            tempstr = tempstr + (char)34 + row[col.Caption].ToString() + (char)34;
        }
    }
    txtstream.WriteLine(tempstr);
    tempstr = "";

}
txtstream.Close();
```

EXCLAMATION DELIMITED HORIZONTAL VIEW

```
String tempstr = "";

Scripting.FileSystemObject fso = new Scripting.FileSystemObject();
Scripting.TextStream txtstream = fso.OpenTextFile(Application.StartupPath +
"\Products.txt",IOMode.ForWriting, True, Tristate.TristateUseDefault);
foreach(System.Data.DataColumn col in dt.Columns)
{
   if (tempstr != "")
   {
      tempstr = tempstr + "!";
   }
   tempstr = tempstr + col.Caption;
}
txtstream.WriteLine(tempstr);
tempstr = "";

foreach(System.Data.DataRow row in dt.Rows)
{
   foreach(System.Data.DataColumn col in dt.Columns)
   {
      if (tempstr != "")
      {
         tempstr = tempstr + "!";
      }
         tempstr = tempstr + (char)34 + row[col.Caption].ToString() + (char)34;
      }
      txtstream.WriteLine(tempstr);
      tempstr = "";

}
txtstream.Close();
```

EXCLAMATION DELIMITED VERTICAL VIEW

```
String tempstr = "";

Scripting.FileSystemObject fso = new Scripting.FileSystemObject();
Scripting.TextStream txtstream = fso.OpenTextFile(Application.StartupPath +
"\Products.txt",IOMode.ForWriting, True, Tristate.TristateUseDefault);
foreach(System.Data.DataColumn col in dt.Columns)
{
```

```
  tempstr = col.Caption;
  foreach(System.Data.DataRow row in dt.Rows)
  {
     if (tempstr != "")
     {
        tempstr = tempstr + "!";
     }
        tempstr = tempstr + (char)34 + row[col.Caption].ToString() + (char)34;
     }
  }
  txtstream.WriteLine(tempstr);
  tempstr = "";

}
txtstream.Close();
```

SEMI-COLON DELIMITED HORIZONTAL VIEW

```
String tempstr = "";

Scripting.FileSystemObject fso = new Scripting.FileSystemObject();
Scripting.TextStream txtstream = fso.OpenTextFile(Application.StartupPath +
"\Products.txt",IOMode.ForWriting, True, Tristate.TristateUseDefault);
foreach(System.Data.DataColumn col in dt.Columns)
{
   if (tempstr != "")
   {
      tempstr = tempstr + ";";
   }
   tempstr = tempstr + col.Caption;
}
txtstream.WriteLine(tempstr);
tempstr = "";

foreach(System.Data.DataRow row in dt.Rows)
{
   foreach(System.Data.DataColumn col in dt.Columns)
   {
      if (tempstr != "")
      {
         tempstr = tempstr + ";";
      }
         tempstr = tempstr + (char)34 + row[col.Caption].ToString() + (char)34;
      }
      txtstream.WriteLine(tempstr);
      tempstr = "";
```

```
}
txtstream.Close();
```

SEMI-COLON DELIMITED VERTICAL VIEW

```
String tempstr = "";

Scripting.FileSystemObject fso = new Scripting.FileSystemObject();
Scripting.TextStream txtstream = fso.OpenTextFile(Application.StartupPath +
"\Products.txt",IOMode.ForWriting, True, Tristate.TristateUseDefault);
foreach(System.Data.DataColumn col in dt.Columns)
{
    tempstr = col.Caption;
    foreach(System.Data.DataRow row in dt.Rows)
    {
        if (tempstr != "")
        {
            tempstr = tempstr + ";";
        }
        tempstr = tempstr + (char)34 + row[col.Caption].ToString() + (char)34;
    }
    txtstream.WriteLine(tempstr);
    tempstr = "";

}
txtstream.Close();
```

TAB DELIMITED HORIZONTAL VIEW

```
String tempstr = "";

Scripting.FileSystemObject fso = new Scripting.FileSystemObject();
Scripting.TextStream txtstream = fso.OpenTextFile(Application.StartupPath +
"\Products.txt",IOMode.ForWriting, True, Tristate.TristateUseDefault);
foreach(System.Data.DataColumn col in dt.Columns)
{
    if (tempstr != "")
    {
        tempstr = tempstr + "\t";
    }
    tempstr = tempstr + col.Caption;
}
txtstream.WriteLine(tempstr);
tempstr = "";
```

```
foreach(System.Data.DataRow row in dt.Rows)
{
    foreach(System.Data.DataColumn col in dt.Columns)
    {
        if (tempstr != "")
        {
            tempstr = tempstr + "\t";
        }
        tempstr = tempstr + (char)34 + row[col.Caption].ToString() + (char)34;
    }
    txtstream.WriteLine(tempstr);
    tempstr = "";

}
txtstream.Close();
```

TAB DELIMITED VERTICAL VIEW

```
String tempstr = "";

Scripting.FileSystemObject fso = new Scripting.FileSystemObject();
Scripting.TextStream txtstream = fso.OpenTextFile(Application.StartupPath +
"\Products.txt",IOMode.ForWriting, True, Tristate.TristateUseDefault);
foreach(System.Data.DataColumn col in dt.Columns)
{
    tempstr = col.Caption;
    foreach(System.Data.DataRow row in dt.Rows)
    {
        if (tempstr != "")
        {
            tempstr = tempstr + "\t";
        }
        tempstr = tempstr + (char)34 + row[col.Caption].ToString() + (char)34;
    }
    txtstream.WriteLine(tempstr);
    tempstr = "";

}
txtstream.Close();
```

TILDE DELIMITED HORIZONTAL VIEW

```
String tempstr = "";
```

```
Scripting.FileSystemObject fso = new Scripting.FileSystemObject();
Scripting.TextStream txtstream = fso.OpenTextFile(Application.StartupPath +
"\Products.txt",IOMode.ForWriting, True, Tristate.TristateUseDefault);
foreach(System.Data.DataColumn col in dt.Columns)
{
   if (tempstr != "")
   {
      tempstr = tempstr + "~";
   }
   tempstr = tempstr + col.Caption;
}
txtstream.WriteLine(tempstr);
tempstr = "";

foreach(System.Data.DataRow row in dt.Rows)
{
   foreach(System.Data.DataColumn col in dt.Columns)
   {
      if (tempstr != "")
      {
         tempstr = tempstr + "~";
      }
      tempstr = tempstr + (char)34 + row[col.Caption].ToString() + (char)34;
   }
   txtstream.WriteLine(tempstr);
   tempstr = "";

}
txtstream.Close();
```

TILDE DELIMITED VERTICAL VIEW

```
String tempstr = "";

Scripting.FileSystemObject fso = new Scripting.FileSystemObject();
Scripting.TextStream txtstream = fso.OpenTextFile(Application.StartupPath +
"\Products.txt",IOMode.ForWriting, True, Tristate.TristateUseDefault);
foreach(System.Data.DataColumn col in dt.Columns)
{
   tempstr = col.Caption;
   foreach(System.Data.DataRow row in dt.Rows)
   {
      if (tempstr != "")
      {
         tempstr = tempstr + "~";
      }
      tempstr = tempstr + (char)34 + row[col.Caption].ToString() + (char)34;
   }
```

```
        }
        txtstream.WriteLine(tempstr);
        tempstr = "";

    }
    txtstream.Close();
```

WORKING EXCEL

The Tale of three ways you can do

it

B ELOW ARE THREE EXAMPLES ON HOW TO WORK WITH EXCEL. The first will need a reference to Microsoft.Office.Interop.Excel.

HORIZONTAL AUTOMATION

```
var oExcel = new Microsoft.Office.Interop.Excel.Application();
oExcel.Visible = true;
var wb = oExcel.Workbooks.Add();
var ws = wb.Worksheets[1];
ws.Name = "Products";

int x = 1;
int y = 2;

foreach(System.Data.DataColumn col in dt.Columns)
{
    ws.Cells[1, x] = col.Caption;
    x=x+1;
}
x = 1;
foreach(System.Data.DataRow row in dt.Rows)
{
    foreach(System.Data.DataColumn col in dt.Columns)
    {
        ws.Cells[y, x] = col.Caption;
```

```
    x=x + 1;
  }
  x = 1;
  y = y + 1;
}
ws.Columns.HorizontalAlignment = -4131;
ws.Columns.AutoFit();
```

VERTICAL AUTOMATION

```
var oExcel = new Microsoft.Office.Interop.Excel.Application();
oExcel.Visible = true;
var wb = oExcel.Workbooks.Add();
var ws = wb.Worksheets[1];
ws.Name = "Products";

int x = 1;
int y = 2;

foreach(System.Data.DataColumn col in dt.Columns)
{
   ws.Cells[x, 1] = col.Caption;
   x=x+1;
}
x = 1;
foreach(System.Data.DataRow row in dt.Rows)
{
   foreach(System.Data.DataColumn col in dt.Columns)
   {
      ws.Cells[x, y] = col.Caption;
      x=x + 1;
   }
   x = 1;
   y = y + 1;
}
ws.Columns.HorizontalAlignment = -4131;
ws.Columns.AutoFit();
```

SPREADSHEET

```
Scripting.FileSystemObject fso = new Scripting.FileSystemObject();
Scripting.TextStream txtstream = fso.OpenTextFile(Application.StartupPath +
"\Products.xml",IOMode.ForWriting, True, Tristate.TristateUseDefault);
txtstream.WriteLine("<?xml version=""1.0""?>");
txtstream.WriteLine("<?mso-application progid=""Excel.Sheet""?>");
txtstream.WriteLine("<Workbook xmlns=""urn:schemas-microsoft-
com:office:spreadsheet"" xmlns:o=""urn:schemas-microsoft-com:office:office""
xmlns:x=""urn:schemas-microsoft-com:office:excel"" xmlns:ss=""urn:schemas-
microsoft-com:office:spreadsheet"" xmlns:html=""http://www.w3.org/TR/REC-
html40"">");
txtstream.WriteLine("   <ExcelWorkbook xmlns=""urn:schemas-microsoft-
com:office:excel"">");
txtstream.WriteLine("        <WindowHeight>11835</WindowHeight>");
txtstream.WriteLine("        <WindowWidth>18960</WindowWidth>");
txtstream.WriteLine("        <WindowTopX>120</WindowTopX>");
txtstream.WriteLine("        <WindowTopY>135</WindowTopY>");
txtstream.WriteLine("        <ProtectStructure>False</ProtectStructure>");
txtstream.WriteLine("        <ProtectWindows>False</ProtectWindows>");
txtstream.WriteLine("   </ExcelWorkbook>");
txtstream.WriteLine("   <Styles>");
txtstream.WriteLine("             <Style ss:ID=""s62"">");
txtstream.WriteLine("                  <Borders/>");
txtstream.WriteLine("                  <Font ss:FontName=""Calibri""
x:Family=""Swiss"" ss:Size=""11"" ss:Color=""#000000"" ss:Bold=""1""/>")
txtstream.WriteLine("             </Style>");
txtstream.WriteLine("             <Style ss:ID=""s63"">");
txtstream.WriteLine("                  <Alignment ss:Horizontal=""Left""
ss:VERTICAL=""Bottom"" ss:Indent=""2""/>");
txtstream.WriteLine("                  <Font ss:FontName=""Verdana""
x:Family=""Swiss"" ss:Size=""7.7"" ss:Color=""#000000""/>")
txtstream.WriteLine("             </Style>");
txtstream.WriteLine("   </Styles>");
txtstream.WriteLine("   <Worksheet ss:Name=""Win32_NetworkAdapter"">");
txtstream.WriteLine("     <Table x:FullColumns=""1"" x:FullRows=""1""
ss:DefaultRowHeight=""24.9375"">");
txtstream.WriteLine("      <Column ss:AutoFitWidth=""1"" ss:Width=""82.5""
ss:Span=""5""/>");
txtstream.WriteLine("     <Row ss:AutoFitHeight=""0"">");
foreach(System.Data.DataColumn col in dt.Columns)
{
   txtstream.WriteLine("        <Cell ss:StyleID=""s62""><Data
ss:Type=""String"">" + col.Caption + "</Data></Cell>");
}
txtstream.WriteLine("     </Row>");
foreach(System.Data.DataRow row in dt.Rows)
{
   txtstream.WriteLine("     <Row ss:AutoFitHeight=""0"">");
   foreach(System.Data.DataColumn col in dt.Columns)
   {
```

```
        txtstream.WriteLine("          <Cell ss:StyleID="""s63"""><Data
ss:Type="""String""">" + row[col.Caption].ToString() + "</Data></Cell>");
    }
    txtstream.WriteLine("      </Row>");
}
txtstream.WriteLine("    </Table>");
txtstream.WriteLine("  </Worksheet>");
txtstream.WriteLine("</Workbook>");
txtstream.Close();
```

HORIZONTAL CSV

```
String tempstr = "";

Scripting.FileSystemObject fso = new Scripting.FileSystemObject();
Scripting.TextStream txtstream = fso.OpenTextFile(Application.StartupPath +
"\Products.csv",IOMode.ForWriting, True, Tristate.TristateUseDefault);
foreach(System.Data.DataColumn col in dt.Columns)
{
    if (tempstr != "")
    {
        tempstr = tempstr + ",";
    }
    tempstr = tempstr + col.Caption;
}
txtstream.WriteLine(tempstr);
tempstr = "";

foreach(System.Data.DataRow row in dt.Rows)
{
    foreach(System.Data.DataColumn col in dt.Columns)
    {
        if (tempstr != "")
        {
            tempstr = tempstr + ",";
        }
        tempstr = tempstr + (char)34 + row[col.Caption].ToString() + (char)34;
    }
    txtstream.WriteLine(tempstr);
    tempstr = "";
}
txtstream.Close();

System.Diagnostics.Process.Start(Application.StartupPath +
"\\Products.csv");
```

VERTICAL CSV

```
String tempstr = "";

Scripting.FileSystemObject fso = new Scripting.FileSystemObject();
Scripting.TextStream txtstream = fso.OpenTextFile(Application.StartupPath +
"\Products.csv",IOMode.ForWriting, True, Tristate.TristateUseDefault);
foreach(System.Data.DataColumn col in dt.Columns)
{
    tempstr = col.Caption;
    foreach(System.Data.DataRow row in dt.Rows)
    {
        if (tempstr != "")
        {
            tempstr = tempstr + ",";
        }
        tempstr = tempstr + (char)34 + row[col.Caption].ToString() + (char)34;
    }
    txtstream.WriteLine(tempstr);
    tempstr = "";

}
txtstream.Close();

System.Diagnostics.Process.Start(Application.StartupPath +
"\\Products.csv");
```

XML FILES

B ELOW ARE XML CODING EXAMPLES IN TEXT AND DOM NOTATION FOR ATTRIBUTE XML, ELEMENT XML, ELEMENT XML FOR XSL AND SCHEMA XML.

TEXT CREATED ATTRIBUTE XML

```
Scripting.FileSystemObject fso = new Scripting.FileSystemObject();
Scripting.TextStream txtstream = fso.OpenTextFile(Application.StartupPath +
"\\Products.xml",IOMode.ForWriting, true, Tristate.TristateUseDefault);
txtstream.WriteLine("<?xml version=\"1.0\" encoding=\"iso-8859-1\"?>");
txtstream.WriteLine("<data>");
foreach(System.Data.DataRow row in dt.Rows)
{
   txtstream.WriteLine("<products>");
   foreach(System.Data.DataColumn col in dt.Columns)
   {
      string tstr = "";
      tstr = "<property name =\"" + col.Caption + "\" ";
      tstr = tstr + " datatype = \"" + col.DataType.Name + "\" ";
      tstr = tstr + " length =\"" + row[col.Caption].ToString().Length + "\" ";
      tstr = tstr + " value =\"" + row[col.Caption] + "\"/>";
      txtstream.WriteLine(tstr);
   }
   txtstream.WriteLine("</products>");
}
txtstream.WriteLine("</data>");
txtstream.Close();
```

DOM CREATED ATTRIBUTE XML

```
XmlDocument xmldoc = new XmlDocument();
XmlProcessingInstruction     pi    =    xmldoc.CreateProcessingInstruction("xml",
"version='1.0' encoding='iso-8895-1'");
XmlNode oRoot = xmldoc.CreateElement("data");
xmldoc.AppendChild(pi);
foreach (System.Data.DataRow row in dt.Rows)
{
   XmlNode oNode = xmldoc.CreateNode(XmlNodeType.Element, "Products", null);
   foreach (System.Data.DataColumn col in dt.Columns)
   {
      XmlNode  oNode1  =  xmldoc.CreateNode(XmlNodeType.Element,  "Property",
null);
      XmlAttribute oatt = xmldoc.CreateAttribute("Name");
      oatt.Value = col.Caption;
      oNode1.Attributes.SetNamedItem(oatt);
      oatt = xmldoc.CreateAttribute("datatype");
      oatt.Value = col.DataType.Name;
      oNode1.Attributes.SetNamedItem(oatt);
      oatt = xmldoc.CreateAttribute("size");
      oatt.Value = row[col.Caption].ToString().Length.ToString();
      oNode1.Attributes.SetNamedItem(oatt);
      oatt = xmldoc.CreateAttribute("value");
      oatt.Value = row[col.Caption].ToString();
      oNode1.Attributes.SetNamedItem(oatt);
      oNode.AppendChild(oNode1);
   }
   oRoot.AppendChild(oNode);
}
xmldoc.AppendChild(oRoot);
xmldoc.Save(Application.StartupPath + "\\Products.xml");
```

TEXT CREATED ELEMENT XML

```
Scripting.FileSystemObject fso = new Scripting.FileSystemObject();
Scripting.TextStream txtstream = fso.OpenTextFile(Application.StartupPath +
"\\Products.xml",IOMode.ForWriting, true, Tristate.TristateUseDefault);
txtstream.WriteLine("<?xml version=\"1.0\" encoding=\"iso-8859-1\"?>");
txtstream.WriteLine("<data>");
foreach(System.Data.DataRow row in dt.Rows)
{
    txtstream.WriteLine("<products>");
    foreach(System.Data.DataColumn col in dt.Columns)
    {
        string tstr = "";
        tstr = "<" + col.Caption + ">";
        tstr = tstr + row[col.Caption];
        tstr = tstr + "</" + col.Caption + ">";
        txtstream.WriteLine(tstr);
    }
    txtstream.WriteLine("</products>");
}
txtstream.WriteLine("</data>");
txtstream.Close();
```

DOM CREATE ELEMENT XML

```
XmlDocument xmldoc = new XmlDocument();
XmlProcessingInstruction pi = xmldoc.CreateProcessingInstruction("xml",
"version='1.0' encoding='iso-8895-1'");
XmlNode oRoot = xmldoc.CreateElement("data");
xmldoc.AppendChild(pi);
foreach (System.Data.DataRow row in dt.Rows)
{
    XmlNode oNode = xmldoc.CreateNode(XmlNodeType.Element, "Products", null);
    foreach (System.Data.DataColumn col in dt.Columns)
    {
        XmlNode oNode1 = xmldoc.CreateNode(XmlNodeType.Element, col.Caption,
null);
        oNode1.InnerText = row[col.Caption].ToString();
        oNode.AppendChild(oNode1);
    }
    oRoot.AppendChild(oNode);
}
xmldoc.AppendChild(oRoot);
xmldoc.Save(Application.StartupPath + "\\Products.xml");
```

TEXT CREATED ELEMENT XML FOR XLS

```
Scripting.FileSystemObject fso = new Scripting.FileSystemObject();
Scripting.TextStream txtstream = fso.OpenTextFile(Application.StartupPath +
"\\Products.xml",IOMode.ForWriting, true, Tristate.TristateUseDefault);
txtstream.WriteLine("<?xml version=\"1.0\" encoding=\"iso-8859-1\"?>");
txtstream.WriteLine("<?xml-stylesheet type='Text/xsl' href=\"Products.xsl\"?>");

txtstream.WriteLine("<data>");
foreach(System.Data.DataRow row in dt.Rows)
{
    txtstream.WriteLine("<products>");
    foreach(System.Data.DataColumn col in dt.Columns)
    {
        string tstr = "";
        tstr = "<" + col.Caption + ">";
        tstr = tstr + row[col.Caption].ToString();
        tstr = tstr + "</" + col.Caption + ">";
        txtstream.WriteLine(tstr);
    }
    txtstream.WriteLine("</products>");
}
txtstream.WriteLine("</data>");
txtstream.Close();
```

DOM CREATE ELEMENT XML FOR XSL

```
XmlDocument xmldoc = new XmlDocument();
XmlProcessingInstruction pi = xmldoc.CreateProcessingInstruction("xml",
"version='1.0' encoding='iso-8895-1'");
XmlProcessingInstruction pii = xmldoc.CreateProcessingInstruction("xml-
stylesheet", "type='text/xsl' href='Products.xsl'");
XmlNode oRoot = xmldoc.CreateElement("data");
xmldoc.AppendChild(pi);
xmldoc.AppendChild(pii);
foreach (System.Data.DataRow row in dt.Rows)
{
    XmlNode oNode = xmldoc.CreateNode(XmlNodeType.Element, "Products", null);
    foreach (System.Data.DataColumn col in dt.Columns)
```

```
    {
        XmlNode  oNode1  =  xmldoc.CreateNode(XmlNodeType.Element,  col.Caption,
null);
        oNode1.InnerText = row[col.Caption].ToString();
        oNode.AppendChild(oNode1);
    }
    oRoot.AppendChild(oNode);
}
xmldoc.AppendChild(oRoot);
xmldoc.Save(Application.StartupPath + "\\Products.xml");
```

TEXT CREATED SCHEMA XML

```
Scripting.FileSystemObject fso = new Scripting.FileSystemObject();
Scripting.TextStream  txtstream  =  fso.OpenTextFile(Application.StartupPath  +
"\\Products.xml",IOMode.ForWriting, true, Tristate.TristateUseDefault);
txtstream.WriteLine("<?xml version=\"1.0\" encoding=\"iso-8859-1\"?>");
txtstream.WriteLine("<data>");
foreach(System.Data.DataRow row in dt.Rows)
{
    txtstream.WriteLine("<products>");
    foreach(System.Data.DataColumn col in dt.Columns)
    {
        string tstr = "";
        tstr = "<" + col.Caption + ">";
        tstr = tstr + row[col.Caption];
        tstr = tstr + "</" + col.Caption + ">";
        txtstream.WriteLine(tstr);
    }
    txtstream.WriteLine("</products>");
}
txtstream.WriteLine("</data>");
txtstream.Close();

ADODB.Recordset rs = new ADODB.Recordset();
rs.ActiveConnection = "Provider=MSDAOSP; Data Source = MSXML2.DSOControl; ";
rs.Open(Application.StartupPath + "\\Products.xml");
rs.Save(Application.StartupPath + "\\ProductsSchema.xml");
```

DOM CREATED SCHEMA XML

```
XmlDocument xmldoc = new XmlDocument();
XmlProcessingInstruction pi = xmldoc.CreateProcessingInstruction("xml",
"version='1.0' encoding='iso-8895-1'");
XmlNode oRoot = xmldoc.CreateElement("data");
xmldoc.AppendChild(pi);
foreach (System.Data.DataRow row in dt.Rows)
{
   XmlNode oNode = xmldoc.CreateNode(XmlNodeType.Element, "Products", null);
   foreach (System.Data.DataColumn col in dt.Columns)
   {
      XmlNode oNode1 = xmldoc.CreateNode(XmlNodeType.Element, col.Caption,
null);
      oNode1.InnerText = row[col.Caption].ToString();
      oNode.AppendChild(oNode1);
   }
   oRoot.AppendChild(oNode);
}
xmldoc.AppendChild(oRoot);
xmldoc.Save(Application.StartupPath + "\\Products.xml");

ADODB.Recordset rs = new ADODB.Recordset();
rs.ActiveConnection = "Provider=MSDAOSP; Data Source = MSXML2.DSOControl; ";
rs.Open(Application.StartupPath + "\\Products.xml");
rs.Save(Application.StartupPath + "\\ProductsSchema.xml");
```

XSL FILES

B ELOW ARE EXAMPLES OF WHAT YOU CAN DO WITH XSL. Views include reports and tables and orientation is for multi-line horizontal, multi-line VERTICAL, single line horizontal and single line VERTICAL.

```
Scripting.FileSystemObject fso = new Scripting.FileSystemObject();
    Scripting.TextStream txtstream = fso.OpenTextFile(Application.StartupPath +
"\\Products.xsl",IOMode.ForWriting, True, Tristate.TristateUseDefault);
    txtstream.WriteLine("<?xml version='1.0' encoding='UTF-8'?>");
    txtstream.WriteLine("<xsl:stylesheet version='1.0'
xmlns:xsl='http://www.w3.org/1999/XSL/Transform'>");
    txtstream.WriteLine("<xsl:template match=\"/\">");
    txtstream.WriteLine("<html>");
    txtstream.WriteLine("<head>");
    txtstream.WriteLine("<title>Products</title>");
    txtstream.WriteLine("</head>");
    txtstream.WriteLine("<body>");
```

For Reports:

```
    txtstream.WriteLine("<table border=""0"" colspacing=""3""
colpadding=""3"">");
```

For Tables:

```
    txtstream.WriteLine("<table border=""1"" colspacing=""3""
colpadding=""3"">");
```

Single Line Horizontal

```
txtstream.WriteLine("<tr>");
foreach(System.Data.DataColumn col in dt.Columns)
{
    txtstream.WriteLine("<th align='left' nowrap='true'>" + col.Caption +
"</th>");
}
txtstream.WriteLine("</tr>");
```

None

```
txtstream.WriteLine("<tr>");
foreach(System.Data.DataColumn col in dt.Columns)
{
    txtstream.WriteLine("<td><xsl:value-of select=\"data/Products/" + col.Caption
+ "\"/></td>");
}
txtstream.WriteLine("</tr>");
```

Button

```
txtstream.WriteLine("<tr>");
foreach(System.Data.DataColumn col in dt.Columns)
{
    txtstream.WriteLine("<td  align='left' nowrap='true'><button
style='width:100%;'><xsl:value-of select=\"data/Products/" + col.Caption  +
"\"/></button></td>");
}
txtstream.WriteLine("</tr>");
```

Combobox

```
txtstream.WriteLine("<tr>");
foreach(System.Data.DataColumn col in dt.Columns)
{
    txtstream.WriteLine("<td                                    align='left'
nowrap='true'><select><option><xsl:attribute        name='value'><xsl:value-of
```

```
select=\"data/Products/"   +   col.Caption      +   "\"/></xsl:attribute><xsl:value-of
select=""data/Products/" + col.Caption  + "\"/></option></select></td>");
    }
    txtstream.WriteLine("</tr>");
```

Div

```
    txtstream.WriteLine("<tr>");
    foreach(System.Data.DataColumn col in dt.Columns)
    {
        txtstream.WriteLine("<td        align='left'    nowrap='true'><div><xsl:value-of
select=\"data/Products/" + col.Caption  + "\"/></div></td>");
    }
    txtstream.WriteLine("</tr>");
```

Link

```
    txtstream.WriteLine("<tr>");
    foreach(System.Data.DataColumn col in dt.Columns)
    {
        txtstream.WriteLine("<td        align='left'    nowrap='true'><a    href='"   +
row[col.Caption].ToString()    +    "'><xsl:value-of    select=\"data/Products/"    +
col.Caption + "\"/></a></td>");
    }
    txtstream.WriteLine("</tr>");
```

Listbox

```
    txtstream.WriteLine("<tr>");
    foreach(System.Data.DataColumn col in dt.Columns)
    {
        txtstream.WriteLine("<td           align='left'          nowrap='true'><select
multiple><option><xsl:attribute                        name='value'><xsl:value-of
select=\"data/Products/"   +   col.Caption      +   "\"/></xsl:attribute><xsl:value-of
select=\"data/Products/" + col.Caption  + "\"/></option></select></td>");
    }
    txtstream.WriteLine("</tr>");
```

```
txtstream.WriteLine("<tr>");
foreach(System.Data.DataColumn col in dt.Columns)
{
    txtstream.WriteLine("<td        align='left'   nowrap='true'><span><xsl:value-of
select=\"data/Products/" + col.Caption  + "\"/></span></td>");
}
txtstream.WriteLine("</tr>");
```

```
txtstream.WriteLine("<tr>");
foreach(System.Data.DataColumn col in dt.Columns)
{
    txtstream.WriteLine("<td  align='left' nowrap='true'><textarea><xsl:value-of
select=\"data/Products/" + col.Caption  + "\"/></textarea></td>");
}
txtstream.WriteLine("</tr>");
```

```
txtstream.WriteLine("<tr>");
foreach(System.Data.DataColumn col in dt.Columns)
{
    txtstream.WriteLine("<td  align='left' nowrap='true'><input
type='text'><xsl:attribute name=""value""><xsl:value-of select=\"data/Products/"
+ col.Caption  + "\"/></xsl:attribute></input></td>");
}
txtstream.WriteLine("</tr>");
```

End code for each routine:

```
txtstream.WriteLine("</table>");
txtstream.WriteLine("</body>");
txtstream.WriteLine("</html>");
txtstream.WriteLine("</xsl:template>");
txtstream.WriteLine("</xsl:stylesheet>");
txtstream.Close();
```

Multi Line Horizontal

```
txtstream.WriteLine("<tr>");
foreach(System.Data.DataColumn col in dt.Columns)
{
    txtstream.WriteLine("<th align='left' nowrap='true'>" + col.Caption +
"</th>");
}
txtstream.WriteLine("</tr>");
```

None

```
txtstream.WriteLine("<xsl:for-each select=\"data/products\">");
txtstream.WriteLine("<tr>");
foreach(System.Data.DataColumn col in dt.Columns)
{
    txtstream.WriteLine("<td><xsl:value-of select=\"" + col.Caption +
"\"/></td>");
}
txtstream.WriteLine("</tr>");
txtstream.WriteLine("</xsl:for-each>");
```

Button

```
txtstream.WriteLine("<xsl:for-each select=\"data/products\">");
txtstream.WriteLine("<tr>");
foreach(System.Data.DataColumn col in dt.Columns)
{
    txtstream.WriteLine("<td align='left' nowrap='true'><button
style='width:100%;'><xsl:value-of select=\"" + col.Caption +
"\"/></button></td>");
}
txtstream.WriteLine("</tr>");
txtstream.WriteLine("</xsl:for-each>");
```

Combobox

```
txtstream.WriteLine("<xsl:for-each select=\"data/products\">");
txtstream.WriteLine("<tr>");
foreach(System.Data.DataColumn col in dt.Columns)
{
```

```
        txtstream.WriteLine("<td                                align='left'
nowrap='true'><select><option><xsl:attribute          name='value'><xsl:value-of
select=\""  +  col.Caption   +  """"/></xsl:attribute><xsl:value-of  select=\""  +
col.Caption + "\"/></option></select></td>");
    }
    txtstream.WriteLine("</tr>");
    txtstream.WriteLine("</xsl:for-each>");
```

```
    txtstream.WriteLine("<xsl:for-each select=\"data/products\">");
    txtstream.WriteLine("<tr>");
    foreach(System.Data.DataColumn col in dt.Columns)
    {
        txtstream.WriteLine("<td        align='left'   nowrap='true'><div><xsl:value-of
select=\"" + col.Caption  + "\"/></div></td>");
    }
    txtstream.WriteLine("</tr>");
    txtstream.WriteLine("</xsl:for-each>");
```

```
    txtstream.WriteLine("<xsl:for-each select=\"data/products\">");
    txtstream.WriteLine("<tr>");
    foreach(System.Data.DataColumn col in dt.Columns)
    {
        txtstream.WriteLine("<td        align='left'   nowrap='true'><a      href='"   +
row[col.Caption].ToString()  +  "'><xsl:value-of   select=\""   +   col.Caption   +
"\"/></a></td>");
    }
    txtstream.WriteLine("</tr>");
    txtstream.WriteLine("</xsl:for-each>");
```

```
    txtstream.WriteLine("<xsl:for-each select=\"data/products\">");
    txtstream.WriteLine("<tr>");
    foreach(System.Data.DataColumn col in dt.Columns)
    {
        txtstream.WriteLine("<td              align='left'         nowrap='true'><select
multiple><option><xsl:attribute     name='value'><xsl:value-of      select=\""      +
```

```
col.Caption     +     "\"/></xsl:attribute><xsl:value-of   select=\""   +   col.Caption     +
"\"/></option></select></td>");
    }
    txtstream.WriteLine("</tr>");
```

Span

```
    txtstream.WriteLine("<xsl:for-each select=\"data/products\">");
    txtstream.WriteLine("<tr>");
    foreach(System.Data.DataColumn col in dt.Columns)
    {
        txtstream.WriteLine("<td        align='left'   nowrap='true'><span><xsl:value-of
select=\"" + col.Caption  + "\"/></span></td>");
    }
    txtstream.WriteLine("</tr>");
    txtstream.WriteLine("</xsl:for-each>");
```

textarea

```
    txtstream.WriteLine("<xsl:for-each select=\"data/products\">");
    txtstream.WriteLine("<tr>");
    foreach(System.Data.DataColumn col in dt.Columns)
    {
        txtstream.WriteLine("<td align='left' nowrap='true'><textarea><xsl:value-of
select=\"" + col.Caption  + "\"/></textarea></td>");
    }
    txtstream.WriteLine("</tr>");
    txtstream.WriteLine("</xsl:for-each>");
```

Textbox

```
    txtstream.WriteLine("<xsl:for-each select=\"data/products\">");
    txtstream.WriteLine("<tr>");
    foreach(System.Data.DataColumn col in dt.Columns)
    {
        txtstream.WriteLine("<td align='left' nowrap='true'><input
type='text'><xsl:attribute name=\"value\"><xsl:value-of select=\"" + col.Caption  +
"\"/></xsl:attribute></input></td>");
    }
    txtstream.WriteLine("</tr>");
    txtstream.WriteLine("</xsl:for-each>");
```

End Code for Each routine.

```
txtstream.WriteLine("</table>");
txtstream.WriteLine("</body>");
txtstream.WriteLine("</html>");
txtstream.WriteLine("</xsl:template>");
txtstream.WriteLine("</xsl:stylesheet>");
txtstream.Close();
```

Single Line VERTICAL

```
foreach(System.Data.DataColumn col in dt.Columns)
{
    txtstream.WriteLine("<tr><th align='left' nowrap='true'>" + col.Caption +
"</th>");
```

None

```
    txtstream.WriteLine("<td><xsl:value-of select=\"data/Products/" + col.Caption
+ "\"/></td></tr>");
```

Button

```
    txtstream.WriteLine("<td  align='left' nowrap='true'><button
style='width:100%;'><xsl:value-of select=\"data/Products/" + col.Caption  +
"\"/></button></td></tr>");
```

Combobox

```
    txtstream.WriteLine("<td                                        align='left'
nowrap='true'><select><option><xsl:attribute            name='value'><xsl:value-of
select=\"data/Products/"    +    col.Caption    +    "\"/></xsl:attribute><xsl:value-of
select=""data/Products/" + col.Caption + "\"/></option></select></td></tr>");
```

Div

```
    txtstream.WriteLine("<td        align='left'    nowrap='true'><div><xsl:value-of
select=\"data/Products/" + col.Caption  + "\"/></div></td></tr>");
```

Link

```
txtstream.WriteLine("<td        align='left'   nowrap='true'><a   href='"   +
row[col.Caption].ToString()    +    "'><xsl:value-of    select=\"data/Products/"    +
col.Caption + "\"/></a></td></tr>");
```

Listbox

```
txtstream.WriteLine("<td             align='left'         nowrap='true'><select
multiple><option><xsl:attribute                    name='value'><xsl:value-of
select=\"data/Products/"   +   col.Caption    +    "\"/></xsl:attribute><xsl:value-of
select=\"data/Products/" + col.Caption + "\"/></option></select></td></tr>");
```

Span

```
txtstream.WriteLine("<td      align='left'  nowrap='true'><span><xsl:value-of
select=\"data/Products/" + col.Caption + "\"/></span></td></tr>");
```

textarea

```
txtstream.WriteLine("<td align='left' nowrap='true'><textarea><xsl:value-of
select=\"data/Products/" + col.Caption + "\"/></textarea></td></tr>");
```

Textbox

```
txtstream.WriteLine("<td align='left' nowrap='true'><input
type='text'><xsl:attribute name=""value""><xsl:value-of select=\"data/Products/"
+ col.Caption + "\"/></xsl:attribute></input></td></tr>");
```


End Code for Each routine.

```
    }
    txtstream.WriteLine("</table>");
    txtstream.WriteLine("</body>");
    txtstream.WriteLine("</html>");
    txtstream.WriteLine("</xsl:template>");
    txtstream.WriteLine("</xsl:stylesheet>");
    txtstream.Close();
```

Multi Line VERTICAL

```
foreach(System.Data.DataColumn col in dt.Columns)
{
    txtstream.WriteLine("<tr><th align='left' nowrap='true'>" + col.Caption +
"</th>");
```

None

```
txtstream.WriteLine("<xsl:for-each select=\"data/products\">");
foreach(System.Data.DataColumn col in dt.Columns)
{
    txtstream.WriteLine("<td><xsl:value-of select=\"" + col.Caption +
"\""/></td>");
}
txtstream.WriteLine("</xsl:for-each>")
txtstream.WriteLine("</tr>");
```

Button

```
txtstream.WriteLine("<xsl:for-each select=\"data/products\">");
foreach(System.Data.DataColumn col in dt.Columns)
{
    txtstream.WriteLine("<td align='left' nowrap='true'><button
style='width:100%;'><xsl:value-of select=\"" + col.Caption +
"\""/></button></td>");
}
txtstream.WriteLine("</tr>");
txtstream.WriteLine("</xsl:for-each>");
```

Combobox

```
txtstream.WriteLine("<xsl:for-each select=\"data/products\">");
foreach(System.Data.DataColumn col in dt.Columns)
{
    txtstream.WriteLine("<td                         align='left'
nowrap='true'><select><option><xsl:attribute           name='value'><xsl:value-of
select=\"" + col.Caption + """"/></xsl:attribute><xsl:value-of select=\"" +
col.Caption + "\""/></option></select></td>");
}
txtstream.WriteLine("</tr>");
txtstream.WriteLine("</xsl:for-each>");
```

Div

```
txtstream.WriteLine("<xsl:for-each select=\"data/products\">");
foreach(System.Data.DataColumn col in dt.Columns)
{
    txtstream.WriteLine("<td        align='left'    nowrap='true'><div><xsl:value-of
select=\"" + col.Caption + "\"/></div></td>");
}
txtstream.WriteLine("</xsl:for-each>");
txtstream.WriteLine("</tr>");
```

Link

```
txtstream.WriteLine("<xsl:for-each select=\"data/products\">");
foreach(System.Data.DataColumn col in dt.Columns)
{
    txtstream.WriteLine("<td        align='left'    nowrap='true'><a    href='"    +
row[col.Caption].ToString() + "'><xsl:value-of    select=\""    +    col.Caption    +
"\"/></a></td>");
}
txtstream.WriteLine("</tr>");
txtstream.WriteLine("</xsl:for-each>");
```

Listbox

```
txtstream.WriteLine("<xsl:for-each select=\"data/products\">");
foreach(System.Data.DataColumn col in dt.Columns)
{
    txtstream.WriteLine("<td                align='left'        nowrap='true'><select
multiple><option><xsl:attribute    name='value'><xsl:value-of    select=\""    +
col.Caption    +    "\"/></xsl:attribute><xsl:value-of  select=\""  +  col.Caption  +
"\"/></option></select></td>");
}
txtstream.WriteLine("</xsl:for-each>");
txtstream.WriteLine("</tr>");
```

Span

```
txtstream.WriteLine("<xsl:for-each select=\"data/products\">");
foreach(System.Data.DataColumn col in dt.Columns)
{
```

```
        txtstream.WriteLine("<td      align='left'   nowrap='true'><span><xsl:value-of
select=\"" + col.Caption  + "\"/></span></td>");
      }
    txtstream.WriteLine("</xsl:for-each>");
    txtstream.WriteLine("</tr>");
```

textarea

```
    txtstream.WriteLine("<xsl:for-each select=\"data/products\">");
    foreach(System.Data.DataColumn col in dt.Columns)
    {
        txtstream.WriteLine("<td align='left' nowrap='true'><textarea><xsl:value-of
select=\"" + col.Caption  + "\"/></textarea></td>");
      }
    txtstream.WriteLine("</xsl:for-each>");
    txtstream.WriteLine("</tr>");
```

Textbox

```
    txtstream.WriteLine("<xsl:for-each select=\"data/products\">");

    foreach(System.Data.DataColumn col in dt.Columns)
    {
        txtstream.WriteLine("<td align='left' nowrap='true'><input
type='text'><xsl:attribute name=\"value\"><xsl:value-of select=\"" + col.Caption  +
"\"/></xsl:attribute></input></td>");
      }
    txtstream.WriteLine("</xsl:for-each>");
    txtstream.WriteLine("</tr>");
```

End Code for Each routine.

```
    txtstream.WriteLine("</table>");
    txtstream.WriteLine("</body>");
    txtstream.WriteLine("</html>");
    txtstream.WriteLine("</xsl:template>");
    txtstream.WriteLine("</xsl:stylesheet>");
    txtstream.Close();
```

STYLESHEETS

Fuel for Thought

THESE ARE SUPPLIED AS IS AND ARE JUST SOME IDEAS I THINK YOU WILL LIKE. DON'T SHOOT THE MESSANGER.

None

```
txtstream.WriteLine("<style type='text/css'>");
txtstream.WriteLine("th");
txtstream.WriteLine("{");
txtstream.WriteLine("    COLOR: white;");
txtstream.WriteLine("}");
txtstream.WriteLine("td");
txtstream.WriteLine("{");
txtstream.WriteLine("    COLOR: white;");
txtstream.WriteLine("}");
txtstream.WriteLine("</style>");
```

Its A Table

```
txtstream.WriteLine("<style type='text/css'>");
txtstream.WriteLine("#itsthetable {");
txtstream.WriteLine("    font-family: Georgia, """"Times New Roman"""",
Times, serif;");
txtstream.WriteLine("    color: #036;");
txtstream.WriteLine("}");

txtstream.WriteLine("caption {");
```

```
txtstream.WriteLine("        font-size: 48px;");
txtstream.WriteLine("        color: #036;");
txtstream.WriteLine("        font-weight: bolder;");
txtstream.WriteLine("        font-variant: small-caps;");
txtstream.WriteLine("}");

txtstream.WriteLine("th {");
txtstream.WriteLine("        font-size: 12px;");
txtstream.WriteLine("        color: #FFF;");
txtstream.WriteLine("        background-color: #06C;");
txtstream.WriteLine("        padding: 8px 4px;");
txtstream.WriteLine("        border-bottom: 1px solid #015ebc;");
txtstream.WriteLine("}");

txtstream.WriteLine("table {");
txtstream.WriteLine("        margin: 0;");
txtstream.WriteLine("        padding: 0;");
txtstream.WriteLine("        border-collapse: collapse;");
txtstream.WriteLine("        border: 1px solid #06C;");
txtstream.WriteLine("        width: 100%");
txtstream.WriteLine("}");

txtstream.WriteLine("#itsthetable th a:link, #itsthetable th a:visited {");
txtstream.WriteLine("        color: #FFF;");
txtstream.WriteLine("        text-decoration: none;");
txtstream.WriteLine("        border-left: 5px solid #FFF;");
txtstream.WriteLine("        padding-left: 3px;");
txtstream.WriteLine("}");

txtstream.WriteLine("th a:hover, #itsthetable th a:active {");
txtstream.WriteLine("        color: #F90;");
txtstream.WriteLine("        text-decoration: line-through;");
txtstream.WriteLine("        border-left: 5px solid #F90;");
txtstream.WriteLine("        padding-left: 3px;");
txtstream.WriteLine("}");

txtstream.WriteLine("tbody th:hover {");
txtstream.WriteLine("        background-image: url(imgs/tbody_hover.gif);");
txtstream.WriteLine("        background-position: bottom;");
txtstream.WriteLine("        background-repeat: repeat-x;");
txtstream.WriteLine("}");

txtstream.WriteLine("td {");
txtstream.WriteLine("        background-color: #f2f2f2;");
txtstream.WriteLine("        padding: 4px;");
txtstream.WriteLine("        font-size: 12px;");
txtstream.WriteLine("}");

txtstream.WriteLine("#itsthetable td:hover {");
txtstream.WriteLine("        background-color: #f8f8f8;");
```

```
txtstream.WriteLine("}");

txtstream.WriteLine("#itsthetable td a:link, #itsthetable td a:visited {");
txtstream.WriteLine("        color: #039;");
txtstream.WriteLine("        text-decoration: none;");
txtstream.WriteLine("        border-left: 3px solid #039;");
txtstream.WriteLine("        padding-left: 3px;");
txtstream.WriteLine("}");

txtstream.WriteLine("#itsthetable td a:hover, #itsthetable td a:active {");
txtstream.WriteLine("        color: #06C;");
txtstream.WriteLine("        text-decoration: line-through;");
txtstream.WriteLine("        border-left: 3px solid #06C;");
txtstream.WriteLine("        padding-left: 3px;");
txtstream.WriteLine("}");

txtstream.WriteLine("#itsthetable th {");
txtstream.WriteLine("        text-align: left;");
txtstream.WriteLine("        width: 150px;");
txtstream.WriteLine("}");

txtstream.WriteLine("#itsthetable tr {");
txtstream.WriteLine("        border-bottom: 1px solid #CCC;");
txtstream.WriteLine("}");

txtstream.WriteLine("#itsthetable thead th {");
txtstream.WriteLine("        background-image: url(imgs/thead_back.gif);");
txtstream.WriteLine("        background-repeat: repeat-x;");
txtstream.WriteLine("        background-color: #06C;");
txtstream.WriteLine("        height: 30px;");
txtstream.WriteLine("        font-size: 18px;");
txtstream.WriteLine("        text-align: center;");
txtstream.WriteLine("        text-shadow: #333 2px 2px;");
txtstream.WriteLine("        border: 2px;");
txtstream.WriteLine("}");

txtstream.WriteLine("#itsthetable tfoot th {");
txtstream.WriteLine("        background-image: url(imgs/tfoot_back.gif);");
txtstream.WriteLine("        background-repeat: repeat-x;");
txtstream.WriteLine("        background-color: #036;");
txtstream.WriteLine("        height: 30px;");
txtstream.WriteLine("        font-size: 28px;");
txtstream.WriteLine("        text-align: center;");
txtstream.WriteLine("        text-shadow: #333 2px 2px;");
txtstream.WriteLine("}");

txtstream.WriteLine("#itsthetable tfoot td {");
txtstream.WriteLine("        background-image: url(imgs/tfoot_back.gif);");
txtstream.WriteLine("        background-repeat: repeat-x;");
```

```
txtstream.WriteLine("        background-color: #036;");
txtstream.WriteLine("        color: FFF;");
txtstream.WriteLine("        height: 30px;");
txtstream.WriteLine("        font-size: 24px;");
txtstream.WriteLine("        text-align: left;");
txtstream.WriteLine("        text-shadow: #333 2px 2px;");
txtstream.WriteLine("}");

txtstream.WriteLine("tbody td a[href=""""""http://www.csslab.cl/""""""] {");
txtstream.WriteLine("        font-weight: bolder;");
txtstream.WriteLine("}");
txtstream.WriteLine("</style>");
```

Black and White Text

```
txtstream.WriteLine("<style type='text/css'>");
txtstream.WriteLine("th");
txtstream.WriteLine("{");
txtstream.WriteLine("    COLOR: white;");
txtstream.WriteLine("    BACKGROUND-COLOR: black;");
txtstream.WriteLine("    FONT-FAMILY: Cambria, serif;");
txtstream.WriteLine("    FONT-SIZE: 12px;");
txtstream.WriteLine("    text-align: left;");
txtstream.WriteLine("    white-Space: nowrap='nowrap';");
txtstream.WriteLine("}");
txtstream.WriteLine("td");
txtstream.WriteLine("{");
txtstream.WriteLine("    COLOR: white;");
txtstream.WriteLine("    BACKGROUND-COLOR: black;");
txtstream.WriteLine("    FONT-FAMILY: Cambria, serif;");
txtstream.WriteLine("    FONT-SIZE: 12px;");
txtstream.WriteLine("    text-align: left;");
txtstream.WriteLine("    white-Space: nowrap='nowrap';");
txtstream.WriteLine("}");
txtstream.WriteLine("div");
txtstream.WriteLine("{");
txtstream.WriteLine("    COLOR: white;");
txtstream.WriteLine("    BACKGROUND-COLOR: black;");
txtstream.WriteLine("    FONT-FAMILY: Cambria, serif;");
txtstream.WriteLine("    FONT-SIZE: 10px;");
txtstream.WriteLine("    text-align: left;");
txtstream.WriteLine("    white-Space: nowrap='nowrap';");
txtstream.WriteLine("}");
txtstream.WriteLine("span");
txtstream.WriteLine("{");
txtstream.WriteLine("    COLOR: white;");
txtstream.WriteLine("    BACKGROUND-COLOR: black;");
txtstream.WriteLine("    FONT-FAMILY: Cambria, serif;");
```

```
txtstream.WriteLine("    FONT-SIZE: 10px;");
txtstream.WriteLine("    text-align: left;");
txtstream.WriteLine("    white-Space: nowrap='nowrap';");
txtstream.WriteLine("    display:inline-block;");
txtstream.WriteLine("    width: 100%;");
txtstream.WriteLine("}");
txtstream.WriteLine("textarea");
txtstream.WriteLine("{");
txtstream.WriteLine("    COLOR: white;");
txtstream.WriteLine("    BACKGROUND-COLOR: black;");
txtstream.WriteLine("    FONT-FAMILY: Cambria, serif;");
txtstream.WriteLine("    FONT-SIZE: 10px;");
txtstream.WriteLine("    text-align: left;");
txtstream.WriteLine("    white-Space: nowrap='nowrap';");
txtstream.WriteLine("    width: 100%;");
txtstream.WriteLine("}");
txtstream.WriteLine("select");
txtstream.WriteLine("{");
txtstream.WriteLine("    COLOR: white;");
txtstream.WriteLine("    BACKGROUND-COLOR: black;");
txtstream.WriteLine("    FONT-FAMILY: Cambria, serif;");
txtstream.WriteLine("    FONT-SIZE: 10px;");
txtstream.WriteLine("    text-align: left;");
txtstream.WriteLine("    white-Space: nowrap='nowrap';");
txtstream.WriteLine("    width: 100%;");
txtstream.WriteLine("}");
txtstream.WriteLine("input");
txtstream.WriteLine("{");
txtstream.WriteLine("    COLOR: white;");
txtstream.WriteLine("    BACKGROUND-COLOR: black;");
txtstream.WriteLine("    FONT-FAMILY: Cambria, serif;");
txtstream.WriteLine("    FONT-SIZE: 12px;");
txtstream.WriteLine("    text-align: left;");
txtstream.WriteLine("    display:table-cell;");
txtstream.WriteLine("    white-Space: nowrap='nowrap';");
txtstream.WriteLine("}");
txtstream.WriteLine("h1 {");
txtstream.WriteLine("color: antiquewhite;");
txtstream.WriteLine("text-shadow: 1px 1px 1px black;");
txtstream.WriteLine("padding: 3px;");
txtstream.WriteLine("text-align: center;");
txtstream.WriteLine("box-shadow: inset 2px 2px 5px rgba(0,0,0,0.5), inset -2px -2px 5px rgba(255,255,255,0.5);");
txtstream.WriteLine("}");
txtstream.WriteLine("</style>");
```

Colored Text

```
txtstream.WriteLine("<style type='text/css'>");
txtstream.WriteLine("th");
txtstream.WriteLine("{");
txtstream.WriteLine("    COLOR: darkred;");
txtstream.WriteLine("    BACKGROUND-COLOR: #eeeeee;");
txtstream.WriteLine("    FONT-FAMILY: Cambria, serif;");
txtstream.WriteLine("    FONT-SIZE: 12px;");
txtstream.WriteLine("    text-align: left;");
txtstream.WriteLine("    white-Space: nowrap='nowrap';");
txtstream.WriteLine("}");
txtstream.WriteLine("td");
txtstream.WriteLine("{");
txtstream.WriteLine("    COLOR: navy;");
txtstream.WriteLine("    BACKGROUND-COLOR: #eeeeee;");
txtstream.WriteLine("    FONT-FAMILY: Cambria, serif;");
txtstream.WriteLine("    FONT-SIZE: 12px;");
txtstream.WriteLine("    text-align: left;");
txtstream.WriteLine("    white-Space: nowrap='nowrap';");
txtstream.WriteLine("}");
txtstream.WriteLine("div");
txtstream.WriteLine("{");
txtstream.WriteLine("    COLOR: white;");
txtstream.WriteLine("    BACKGROUND-COLOR: navy;");
txtstream.WriteLine("    FONT-FAMILY: Cambria, serif;");
txtstream.WriteLine("    FONT-SIZE: 10px;");
txtstream.WriteLine("    text-align: left;");
txtstream.WriteLine("    white-Space: nowrap='nowrap';");
txtstream.WriteLine("}");
txtstream.WriteLine("span");
txtstream.WriteLine("{");
txtstream.WriteLine("    COLOR: white;");
txtstream.WriteLine("    BACKGROUND-COLOR: navy;");
txtstream.WriteLine("    FONT-FAMILY: Cambria, serif;");
txtstream.WriteLine("    FONT-SIZE: 10px;");
txtstream.WriteLine("    text-align: left;");
txtstream.WriteLine("    white-Space: nowrap='nowrap';");
txtstream.WriteLine("    display:inline-block;");
txtstream.WriteLine("    width: 100%;");
txtstream.WriteLine("}");
txtstream.WriteLine("textarea");
txtstream.WriteLine("{");
txtstream.WriteLine("    COLOR: white;");
txtstream.WriteLine("    BACKGROUND-COLOR: navy;");
txtstream.WriteLine("    FONT-FAMILY: Cambria, serif;");
txtstream.WriteLine("    FONT-SIZE: 10px;");
txtstream.WriteLine("    text-align: left;");
txtstream.WriteLine("    white-Space: nowrap='nowrap';");
txtstream.WriteLine("    width: 100%;");
txtstream.WriteLine("}");
txtstream.WriteLine("select");
```

```
txtstream.WriteLine("{");
txtstream.WriteLine("    COLOR: white;");
txtstream.WriteLine("    BACKGROUND-COLOR: navy;");
txtstream.WriteLine("    FONT-FAMILY: Cambria, serif;");
txtstream.WriteLine("    FONT-SIZE: 10px;");
txtstream.WriteLine("    text-align: left;");
txtstream.WriteLine("    white-Space: nowrap='nowrap';");
txtstream.WriteLine("    width: 100%;");
txtstream.WriteLine("}");
txtstream.WriteLine("input");
txtstream.WriteLine("{");
txtstream.WriteLine("    COLOR: white;");
txtstream.WriteLine("    BACKGROUND-COLOR: navy;");
txtstream.WriteLine("    FONT-FAMILY: Cambria, serif;");
txtstream.WriteLine("    FONT-SIZE: 12px;");
txtstream.WriteLine("    text-align: left;");
txtstream.WriteLine("    display:table-cell;");
txtstream.WriteLine("    white-Space: nowrap='nowrap';");
txtstream.WriteLine("}");
txtstream.WriteLine("h1 {");
txtstream.WriteLine("color: antiquewhite;");
txtstream.WriteLine("text-shadow: 1px 1px 1px black;");
txtstream.WriteLine("padding: 3px;");
txtstream.WriteLine("text-align: center;");
txtstream.WriteLine("box-shadow: inset 2px 2px 5px rgba(0,0,0,0.5), inset -2px -
2px 5px rgba(255,255,255,0.5);");
txtstream.WriteLine("}");
txtstream.WriteLine("</style>");
```

Oscillating Row Colors

```
txtstream.WriteLine("<style type='text/css'>");
txtstream.WriteLine("th");
txtstream.WriteLine("{");
txtstream.WriteLine("    COLOR: white;");
txtstream.WriteLine("    BACKGROUND-COLOR: navy;");
txtstream.WriteLine("    FONT-FAMILY: Cambria, serif;");
txtstream.WriteLine("    FONT-SIZE: 12px;");
txtstream.WriteLine("    text-align: left;");
txtstream.WriteLine("    white-Space: nowrap='nowrap';");
txtstream.WriteLine("}");
txtstream.WriteLine("td");
txtstream.WriteLine("{");
txtstream.WriteLine("    COLOR: navy;");
txtstream.WriteLine("    FONT-FAMILY: Cambria, serif;");
txtstream.WriteLine("    FONT-SIZE: 12px;");
txtstream.WriteLine("    text-align: left;");
```

```
txtstream.WriteLine(" white-Space: nowrap='nowrap';");
txtstream.WriteLine("}");
txtstream.WriteLine("div");
txtstream.WriteLine("{");
txtstream.WriteLine(" COLOR: navy;");
txtstream.WriteLine(" FONT-FAMILY: Cambria, serif;");
txtstream.WriteLine(" FONT-SIZE: 12px;");
txtstream.WriteLine(" text-align: left;");
txtstream.WriteLine(" white-Space: nowrap='nowrap';");
txtstream.WriteLine("}");
txtstream.WriteLine("span");
txtstream.WriteLine("{");
txtstream.WriteLine(" COLOR: navy;");
txtstream.WriteLine(" FONT-FAMILY: Cambria, serif;");
txtstream.WriteLine(" FONT-SIZE: 12px;");
txtstream.WriteLine(" text-align: left;");
txtstream.WriteLine(" white-Space: nowrap='nowrap';");
txtstream.WriteLine(" width: 100%;");
txtstream.WriteLine("}");
txtstream.WriteLine("textarea");
txtstream.WriteLine("{");
txtstream.WriteLine(" COLOR: navy;");
txtstream.WriteLine(" FONT-FAMILY: Cambria, serif;");
txtstream.WriteLine(" FONT-SIZE: 12px;");
txtstream.WriteLine(" text-align: left;");
txtstream.WriteLine(" white-Space: nowrap='nowrap';");
txtstream.WriteLine(" display:inline-block;");
txtstream.WriteLine(" width: 100%;");
txtstream.WriteLine("}");
txtstream.WriteLine("select");
txtstream.WriteLine("{");
txtstream.WriteLine(" COLOR: navy;");
txtstream.WriteLine(" FONT-FAMILY: Cambria, serif;");
txtstream.WriteLine(" FONT-SIZE: 10px;");
txtstream.WriteLine(" text-align: left;");
txtstream.WriteLine(" white-Space: nowrap='nowrap';");
txtstream.WriteLine(" display:inline-block;");
txtstream.WriteLine(" width: 100%;");
txtstream.WriteLine("}");
txtstream.WriteLine("input");
txtstream.WriteLine("{");
txtstream.WriteLine(" COLOR: navy;");
txtstream.WriteLine(" FONT-FAMILY: Cambria, serif;");
txtstream.WriteLine(" FONT-SIZE: 12px;");
txtstream.WriteLine(" text-align: left;");
txtstream.WriteLine(" display:table-cell;");
txtstream.WriteLine(" white-Space: nowrap='nowrap';");
txtstream.WriteLine("}");
txtstream.WriteLine("h1 {");
txtstream.WriteLine("color: antiquewhite;");
```

```
txtstream.WriteLine("text-shadow: 1px 1px 1px black;");
txtstream.WriteLine("padding: 3px;");
txtstream.WriteLine("text-align: center;");
txtstream.WriteLine("box-shadow: inset 2px 2px 5px rgba(0,0,0,0.5), inset -2px -
2px 5px rgba(255,255,255,0.5);");
txtstream.WriteLine("}");
txtstream.WriteLine("tr:nth-child(even){background-color:#f2f2f2;}");
txtstream.WriteLine("tr:nth-child(odd){background-color:#cccccc;
color:#f2f2f2;}");
txtstream.WriteLine("</style>");
```

Ghost Decorated

```
txtstream.WriteLine("<style type='text/css'>");
txtstream.WriteLine("th");
txtstream.WriteLine("{");
txtstream.WriteLine("   COLOR: black;");
txtstream.WriteLine("   BACKGROUND-COLOR: white;");
txtstream.WriteLine("   FONT-FAMILY: Cambria, serif;");
txtstream.WriteLine("   FONT-SIZE: 12px;");
txtstream.WriteLine("   text-align: left;");
txtstream.WriteLine("   white-Space: nowrap='nowrap';");
txtstream.WriteLine("}");
txtstream.WriteLine("td");
txtstream.WriteLine("{");
txtstream.WriteLine("   COLOR: black;");
txtstream.WriteLine("   BACKGROUND-COLOR: white;");
txtstream.WriteLine("   FONT-FAMILY: Cambria, serif;");
txtstream.WriteLine("   FONT-SIZE: 12px;");
txtstream.WriteLine("   text-align: left;");
txtstream.WriteLine("   white-Space: nowrap='nowrap';");
txtstream.WriteLine("}");
txtstream.WriteLine("div");
txtstream.WriteLine("{");
txtstream.WriteLine("   COLOR: black;");
txtstream.WriteLine("   BACKGROUND-COLOR: white;");
txtstream.WriteLine("   FONT-FAMILY: Cambria, serif;");
txtstream.WriteLine("   FONT-SIZE: 10px;");
txtstream.WriteLine("   text-align: left;");
txtstream.WriteLine("   white-Space: nowrap='nowrap';");
txtstream.WriteLine("}");
txtstream.WriteLine("span");
txtstream.WriteLine("{");
txtstream.WriteLine("   COLOR: black;");
txtstream.WriteLine("   BACKGROUND-COLOR: white;");
txtstream.WriteLine("   FONT-FAMILY: Cambria, serif;");
txtstream.WriteLine("   FONT-SIZE: 10px;");
txtstream.WriteLine("   text-align: left;");
txtstream.WriteLine("   white-Space: nowrap='nowrap';");
```

```
txtstream.WriteLine("    display:inline-block;");
txtstream.WriteLine("    width: 100%;");
txtstream.WriteLine("}");
txtstream.WriteLine("textarea");
txtstream.WriteLine("{");
txtstream.WriteLine("    COLOR: black;");
txtstream.WriteLine("    BACKGROUND-COLOR: white;");
txtstream.WriteLine("    FONT-FAMILY: Cambria, serif;");
txtstream.WriteLine("    FONT-SIZE: 10px;");
txtstream.WriteLine("    text-align: left;");
txtstream.WriteLine("    white-Space: nowrap='nowrap';");
txtstream.WriteLine("    width: 100%;");
txtstream.WriteLine("}");
txtstream.WriteLine("select");
txtstream.WriteLine("{");
txtstream.WriteLine("    COLOR: black;");
txtstream.WriteLine("    BACKGROUND-COLOR: white;");
txtstream.WriteLine("    FONT-FAMILY: Cambria, serif;");
txtstream.WriteLine("    FONT-SIZE: 10px;");
txtstream.WriteLine("    text-align: left;");
txtstream.WriteLine("    white-Space: nowrap='nowrap';");
txtstream.WriteLine("    width: 100%;");
txtstream.WriteLine("}");
txtstream.WriteLine("input");
txtstream.WriteLine("{");
txtstream.WriteLine("    COLOR: black;");
txtstream.WriteLine("    BACKGROUND-COLOR: white;");
txtstream.WriteLine("    FONT-FAMILY: Cambria, serif;");
txtstream.WriteLine("    FONT-SIZE: 12px;");
txtstream.WriteLine("    text-align: left;");
txtstream.WriteLine("    display:table-cell;");
txtstream.WriteLine("    white-Space: nowrap='nowrap';");
txtstream.WriteLine("}");
txtstream.WriteLine("h1 {");
txtstream.WriteLine("color: antiquewhite;");
txtstream.WriteLine("text-shadow: 1px 1px 1px black;");
txtstream.WriteLine("padding: 3px;");
txtstream.WriteLine("text-align: center;");
txtstream.WriteLine("box-shadow: inset 2px 2px 5px rgba(0,0,0,0.5), inset -2px -
2px 5px rgba(255,255,255,0.5);");
txtstream.WriteLine("}");
txtstream.WriteLine("</style>");
```

3D

```
txtstream.WriteLine("<style type='text/css'>");
txtstream.WriteLine("body");
txtstream.WriteLine("{");
txtstream.WriteLine("    PADDING-RIGHT: 0px;");
```

```
txtstream.WriteLine("    PADDING-LEFT: 0px;");
txtstream.WriteLine("    PADDING-BOTTOM: 0px;");
txtstream.WriteLine("    MARGIN: 0px;");
txtstream.WriteLine("    COLOR: #333;");
txtstream.WriteLine("    PADDING-TOP: 0px;");
txtstream.WriteLine("    FONT-FAMILY: verdana, arial, helvetica, sans-serif;");
txtstream.WriteLine("}");
txtstream.WriteLine("table");
txtstream.WriteLine("{");
txtstream.WriteLine("    BORDER-RIGHT: #999999 3px solid;");
txtstream.WriteLine("    PADDING-RIGHT: 6px;");
txtstream.WriteLine("    PADDING-LEFT: 6px;");
txtstream.WriteLine("    FONT-WEIGHT: Bold;");
txtstream.WriteLine("    FONT-SIZE: 14px;");
txtstream.WriteLine("    PADDING-BOTTOM: 6px;");
txtstream.WriteLine("    COLOR: Peru;");
txtstream.WriteLine("    LINE-HEIGHT: 14px;");
txtstream.WriteLine("    PADDING-TOP: 6px;");
txtstream.WriteLine("    BORDER-BOTTOM: #999 1px solid;");
txtstream.WriteLine("    BACKGROUND-COLOR: #eeeeee;");
txtstream.WriteLine("    FONT-FAMILY: verdana, arial, helvetica, sans-serif;");
txtstream.WriteLine("    FONT-SIZE: 12px;");
txtstream.WriteLine("}");
txtstream.WriteLine("th");
txtstream.WriteLine("{");
txtstream.WriteLine("    BORDER-RIGHT: #999999 3px solid;");
txtstream.WriteLine("    PADDING-RIGHT: 6px;");
txtstream.WriteLine("    PADDING-LEFT: 6px;");
txtstream.WriteLine("    FONT-WEIGHT: Bold;");
txtstream.WriteLine("    FONT-SIZE: 14px;");
txtstream.WriteLine("    PADDING-BOTTOM: 6px;");
txtstream.WriteLine("    COLOR: darkred;");
txtstream.WriteLine("    LINE-HEIGHT: 14px;");
txtstream.WriteLine("    PADDING-TOP: 6px;");
txtstream.WriteLine("    BORDER-BOTTOM: #999 1px solid;");
txtstream.WriteLine("    BACKGROUND-COLOR: #eeeeee;");
txtstream.WriteLine("    FONT-FAMILY: Cambria, serif;");
txtstream.WriteLine("    FONT-SIZE: 12px;");
txtstream.WriteLine("    text-align: left;");
txtstream.WriteLine("    white-Space: nowrap='nowrap';");
txtstream.WriteLine("}");
txtstream.WriteLine(".th");
txtstream.WriteLine("{");
txtstream.WriteLine("    BORDER-RIGHT: #999999 2px solid;");
txtstream.WriteLine("    PADDING-RIGHT: 6px;");
txtstream.WriteLine("    PADDING-LEFT: 6px;");
txtstream.WriteLine("    FONT-WEIGHT: Bold;");
txtstream.WriteLine("    PADDING-BOTTOM: 6px;");
txtstream.WriteLine("    COLOR: black;");
txtstream.WriteLine("    PADDING-TOP: 6px;");
```

```
txtstream.WriteLine("   BORDER-BOTTOM: #999 2px solid;");
txtstream.WriteLine("   BACKGROUND-COLOR: #eeeeee;");
txtstream.WriteLine("   FONT-FAMILY: Cambria, serif;");
txtstream.WriteLine("   FONT-SIZE: 10px;");
txtstream.WriteLine("   text-align: right;");
txtstream.WriteLine("   white-Space: nowrap='nowrap';");
txtstream.WriteLine("}");
txtstream.WriteLine("td");
txtstream.WriteLine("{");
txtstream.WriteLine("   BORDER-RIGHT: #999999 3px solid;");
txtstream.WriteLine("   PADDING-RIGHT: 6px;");
txtstream.WriteLine("   PADDING-LEFT: 6px;");
txtstream.WriteLine("   FONT-WEIGHT: Normal;");
txtstream.WriteLine("   PADDING-BOTTOM: 6px;");
txtstream.WriteLine("   COLOR: navy;");
txtstream.WriteLine("   LINE-HEIGHT: 14px;");
txtstream.WriteLine("   PADDING-TOP: 6px;");
txtstream.WriteLine("   BORDER-BOTTOM: #999 1px solid;");
txtstream.WriteLine("   BACKGROUND-COLOR: #eeeeee;");
txtstream.WriteLine("   FONT-FAMILY: Cambria, serif;");
txtstream.WriteLine("   FONT-SIZE: 12px;");
txtstream.WriteLine("   text-align: left;");
txtstream.WriteLine("   white-Space: nowrap='nowrap';");
txtstream.WriteLine("}");
txtstream.WriteLine("div");
txtstream.WriteLine("{");
txtstream.WriteLine("   BORDER-RIGHT: #999999 3px solid;");
txtstream.WriteLine("   PADDING-RIGHT: 6px;");
txtstream.WriteLine("   PADDING-LEFT: 6px;");
txtstream.WriteLine("   FONT-WEIGHT: Normal;");
txtstream.WriteLine("   PADDING-BOTTOM: 6px;");
txtstream.WriteLine("   COLOR: white;");
txtstream.WriteLine("   PADDING-TOP: 6px;");
txtstream.WriteLine("   BORDER-BOTTOM: #999 1px solid;");
txtstream.WriteLine("   BACKGROUND-COLOR: navy;");
txtstream.WriteLine("   FONT-FAMILY: Cambria, serif;");
txtstream.WriteLine("   FONT-SIZE: 10px;");
txtstream.WriteLine("   text-align: left;");
txtstream.WriteLine("   white-Space: nowrap='nowrap';");
txtstream.WriteLine("}");
txtstream.WriteLine("span");
txtstream.WriteLine("{");
txtstream.WriteLine("   BORDER-RIGHT: #999999 3px solid;");
txtstream.WriteLine("   PADDING-RIGHT: 3px;");
txtstream.WriteLine("   PADDING-LEFT: 3px;");
txtstream.WriteLine("   FONT-WEIGHT: Normal;");
txtstream.WriteLine("   PADDING-BOTTOM: 3px;");
txtstream.WriteLine("   COLOR: white;");
txtstream.WriteLine("   PADDING-TOP: 3px;");
txtstream.WriteLine("   BORDER-BOTTOM: #999 1px solid;");
```

```
txtstream.WriteLine("    BACKGROUND-COLOR: navy;");
txtstream.WriteLine("    FONT-FAMILY: Cambria, serif;");
txtstream.WriteLine("    FONT-SIZE: 10px;");
txtstream.WriteLine("    text-align: left;");
txtstream.WriteLine("    white-Space: nowrap='nowrap';");
txtstream.WriteLine("    display:inline-block;");
txtstream.WriteLine("    width: 100%;");
txtstream.WriteLine("}");
txtstream.WriteLine("textarea");
txtstream.WriteLine("{");
txtstream.WriteLine("    BORDER-RIGHT: #999999 3px solid;");
txtstream.WriteLine("    PADDING-RIGHT: 3px;");
txtstream.WriteLine("    PADDING-LEFT: 3px;");
txtstream.WriteLine("    FONT-WEIGHT: Normal;");
txtstream.WriteLine("    PADDING-BOTTOM: 3px;");
txtstream.WriteLine("    COLOR: white;");
txtstream.WriteLine("    PADDING-TOP: 3px;");
txtstream.WriteLine("    BORDER-BOTTOM: #999 1px solid;");
txtstream.WriteLine("    BACKGROUND-COLOR: navy;");
txtstream.WriteLine("    FONT-FAMILY: Cambria, serif;");
txtstream.WriteLine("    FONT-SIZE: 10px;");
txtstream.WriteLine("    text-align: left;");
txtstream.WriteLine("    white-Space: nowrap='nowrap';");
txtstream.WriteLine("    width: 100%;");
txtstream.WriteLine("}");
txtstream.WriteLine("select");
txtstream.WriteLine("{");
txtstream.WriteLine("    BORDER-RIGHT: #999999 3px solid;");
txtstream.WriteLine("    PADDING-RIGHT: 6px;");
txtstream.WriteLine("    PADDING-LEFT: 6px;");
txtstream.WriteLine("    FONT-WEIGHT: Normal;");
txtstream.WriteLine("    PADDING-BOTTOM: 6px;");
txtstream.WriteLine("    COLOR: white;");
txtstream.WriteLine("    PADDING-TOP: 6px;");
txtstream.WriteLine("    BORDER-BOTTOM: #999 1px solid;");
txtstream.WriteLine("    BACKGROUND-COLOR: navy;");
txtstream.WriteLine("    FONT-FAMILY: Cambria, serif;");
txtstream.WriteLine("    FONT-SIZE: 10px;");
txtstream.WriteLine("    text-align: left;");
txtstream.WriteLine("    white-Space: nowrap='nowrap';");
txtstream.WriteLine("    width: 100%;");
txtstream.WriteLine("}");
txtstream.WriteLine("input");
txtstream.WriteLine("{");
txtstream.WriteLine("    BORDER-RIGHT: #999999 3px solid;");
txtstream.WriteLine("    PADDING-RIGHT: 3px;");
txtstream.WriteLine("    PADDING-LEFT: 3px;");
txtstream.WriteLine("    FONT-WEIGHT: Bold;");
txtstream.WriteLine("    PADDING-BOTTOM: 3px;");
txtstream.WriteLine("    COLOR: white;");
```

```
txtstream.WriteLine("   PADDING-TOP: 3px;");
txtstream.WriteLine("   BORDER-BOTTOM: #999 1px solid;");
txtstream.WriteLine("   BACKGROUND-COLOR: navy;");
txtstream.WriteLine("   FONT-FAMILY: Cambria, serif;");
txtstream.WriteLine("   FONT-SIZE: 12px;");
txtstream.WriteLine("   text-align: left;");
txtstream.WriteLine("   display:table-cell;");
txtstream.WriteLine("   white-Space: nowrap='nowrap';");
txtstream.WriteLine("   width: 100%;");
txtstream.WriteLine("}");
txtstream.WriteLine("h1 {");
txtstream.WriteLine("color: antiquewhite;");
txtstream.WriteLine("text-shadow: 1px 1px 1px black;");
txtstream.WriteLine("padding: 3px;");
txtstream.WriteLine("text-align: center;");
txtstream.WriteLine("box-shadow: inset 2px 2px 5px rgba(0,0,0,0.5), inset -2px -2px 5px rgba(255,255,255,0.5);");
txtstream.WriteLine("}");
txtstream.WriteLine("</style>");
```

Shadow Box

```
txtstream.WriteLine("<style type='text/css'>");
txtstream.WriteLine("body");
txtstream.WriteLine("{");
txtstream.WriteLine("   PADDING-RIGHT: 0px;");
txtstream.WriteLine("   PADDING-LEFT: 0px;");
txtstream.WriteLine("   PADDING-BOTTOM: 0px;");
txtstream.WriteLine("   MARGIN: 0px;");
txtstream.WriteLine("   COLOR: #333;");
txtstream.WriteLine("   PADDING-TOP: 0px;");
txtstream.WriteLine("   FONT-FAMILY: verdana, arial, helvetica, sans-serif;");
txtstream.WriteLine("}");
txtstream.WriteLine("table");
txtstream.WriteLine("{");
txtstream.WriteLine("   BORDER-RIGHT: #999999 1px solid;");
txtstream.WriteLine("   PADDING-RIGHT: 1px;");
txtstream.WriteLine("   PADDING-LEFT: 1px;");
txtstream.WriteLine("   PADDING-BOTTOM: 1px;");
txtstream.WriteLine("   LINE-HEIGHT: 8px;");
txtstream.WriteLine("   PADDING-TOP: 1px;");
txtstream.WriteLine("   BORDER-BOTTOM: #999 1px solid;");
txtstream.WriteLine("   BACKGROUND-COLOR: #eeeeee;");
txtstream.WriteLine("
filter:progid:DXImageTransform.Microsoft.Shadow(color='silver', Direction=135,
Strength=16)");
txtstream.WriteLine("}");
txtstream.WriteLine("th");
txtstream.WriteLine("{");
```

```
txtstream.WriteLine("    BORDER-RIGHT: #999999 3px solid;");
txtstream.WriteLine("    PADDING-RIGHT: 6px;");
txtstream.WriteLine("    PADDING-LEFT: 6px;");
txtstream.WriteLine("    FONT-WEIGHT: Bold;");
txtstream.WriteLine("    FONT-SIZE: 14px;");
txtstream.WriteLine("    PADDING-BOTTOM: 6px;");
txtstream.WriteLine("    COLOR: darkred;");
txtstream.WriteLine("    LINE-HEIGHT: 14px;");
txtstream.WriteLine("    PADDING-TOP: 6px;");
txtstream.WriteLine("    BORDER-BOTTOM: #999 1px solid;");
txtstream.WriteLine("    BACKGROUND-COLOR: #eeeeee;");
txtstream.WriteLine("    FONT-FAMILY: Cambria, serif;");
txtstream.WriteLine("    FONT-SIZE: 12px;");
txtstream.WriteLine("    text-align: left;");
txtstream.WriteLine("    white-Space: nowrap='nowrap';");
txtstream.WriteLine("}");
txtstream.WriteLine(".th");
txtstream.WriteLine("{");
txtstream.WriteLine("    BORDER-RIGHT: #999999 2px solid;");
txtstream.WriteLine("    PADDING-RIGHT: 6px;");
txtstream.WriteLine("    PADDING-LEFT: 6px;");
txtstream.WriteLine("    FONT-WEIGHT: Bold;");
txtstream.WriteLine("    PADDING-BOTTOM: 6px;");
txtstream.WriteLine("    COLOR: black;");
txtstream.WriteLine("    PADDING-TOP: 6px;");
txtstream.WriteLine("    BORDER-BOTTOM: #999 2px solid;");
txtstream.WriteLine("    BACKGROUND-COLOR: #eeeeee;");
txtstream.WriteLine("    FONT-FAMILY: Cambria, serif;");
txtstream.WriteLine("    FONT-SIZE: 10px;");
txtstream.WriteLine("    text-align: right;");
txtstream.WriteLine("    white-Space: nowrap='nowrap';");
txtstream.WriteLine("}");
txtstream.WriteLine("td");
txtstream.WriteLine("{");
txtstream.WriteLine("    BORDER-RIGHT: #999999 3px solid;");
txtstream.WriteLine("    PADDING-RIGHT: 6px;");
txtstream.WriteLine("    PADDING-LEFT: 6px;");
txtstream.WriteLine("    FONT-WEIGHT: Normal;");
txtstream.WriteLine("    PADDING-BOTTOM: 6px;");
txtstream.WriteLine("    COLOR: navy;");
txtstream.WriteLine("    LINE-HEIGHT: 14px;");
txtstream.WriteLine("    PADDING-TOP: 6px;");
txtstream.WriteLine("    BORDER-BOTTOM: #999 1px solid;");
txtstream.WriteLine("    BACKGROUND-COLOR: #eeeeee;");
txtstream.WriteLine("    FONT-FAMILY: Cambria, serif;");
txtstream.WriteLine("    FONT-SIZE: 12px;");
txtstream.WriteLine("    text-align: left;");
txtstream.WriteLine("    white-Space: nowrap='nowrap';");
txtstream.WriteLine("}");
txtstream.WriteLine("div");
```

```
txtstream.WriteLine("{");
txtstream.WriteLine("    BORDER-RIGHT: #999999 3px solid;");
txtstream.WriteLine("    PADDING-RIGHT: 6px;");
txtstream.WriteLine("    PADDING-LEFT: 6px;");
txtstream.WriteLine("    FONT-WEIGHT: Normal;");
txtstream.WriteLine("    PADDING-BOTTOM: 6px;");
txtstream.WriteLine("    COLOR: white;");
txtstream.WriteLine("    PADDING-TOP: 6px;");
txtstream.WriteLine("    BORDER-BOTTOM: #999 1px solid;");
txtstream.WriteLine("    BACKGROUND-COLOR: navy;");
txtstream.WriteLine("    FONT-FAMILY: Cambria, serif;");
txtstream.WriteLine("    FONT-SIZE: 10px;");
txtstream.WriteLine("    text-align: left;");
txtstream.WriteLine("    white-Space: nowrap='nowrap';");
txtstream.WriteLine("}");
txtstream.WriteLine("span");
txtstream.WriteLine("{");
txtstream.WriteLine("    BORDER-RIGHT: #999999 3px solid;");
txtstream.WriteLine("    PADDING-RIGHT: 3px;");
txtstream.WriteLine("    PADDING-LEFT: 3px;");
txtstream.WriteLine("    FONT-WEIGHT: Normal;");
txtstream.WriteLine("    PADDING-BOTTOM: 3px;");
txtstream.WriteLine("    COLOR: white;");
txtstream.WriteLine("    PADDING-TOP: 3px;");
txtstream.WriteLine("    BORDER-BOTTOM: #999 1px solid;");
txtstream.WriteLine("    BACKGROUND-COLOR: navy;");
txtstream.WriteLine("    FONT-FAMILY: Cambria, serif;");
txtstream.WriteLine("    FONT-SIZE: 10px;");
txtstream.WriteLine("    text-align: left;");
txtstream.WriteLine("    white-Space: nowrap='nowrap';");
txtstream.WriteLine("    display: inline-block;");
txtstream.WriteLine("    width: 100%;");
txtstream.WriteLine("}");
txtstream.WriteLine("textarea");
txtstream.WriteLine("{");
txtstream.WriteLine("    BORDER-RIGHT: #999999 3px solid;");
txtstream.WriteLine("    PADDING-RIGHT: 3px;");
txtstream.WriteLine("    PADDING-LEFT: 3px;");
txtstream.WriteLine("    FONT-WEIGHT: Normal;");
txtstream.WriteLine("    PADDING-BOTTOM: 3px;");
txtstream.WriteLine("    COLOR: white;");
txtstream.WriteLine("    PADDING-TOP: 3px;");
txtstream.WriteLine("    BORDER-BOTTOM: #999 1px solid;");
txtstream.WriteLine("    BACKGROUND-COLOR: navy;");
txtstream.WriteLine("    FONT-FAMILY: Cambria, serif;");
txtstream.WriteLine("    FONT-SIZE: 10px;");
txtstream.WriteLine("    text-align: left;");
txtstream.WriteLine("    white-Space: nowrap='nowrap';");
txtstream.WriteLine("    width: 100%;");
txtstream.WriteLine("}");
```

```
txtstream.WriteLine("select");
txtstream.WriteLine("{");
txtstream.WriteLine("    BORDER-RIGHT: #999999 3px solid;");
txtstream.WriteLine("    PADDING-RIGHT: 6px;");
txtstream.WriteLine("    PADDING-LEFT: 6px;");
txtstream.WriteLine("    FONT-WEIGHT: Normal;");
txtstream.WriteLine("    PADDING-BOTTOM: 6px;");
txtstream.WriteLine("    COLOR: white;");
txtstream.WriteLine("    PADDING-TOP: 6px;");
txtstream.WriteLine("    BORDER-BOTTOM: #999 1px solid;");
txtstream.WriteLine("    BACKGROUND-COLOR: navy;");
txtstream.WriteLine("    FONT-FAMILY:  Cambria, serif;");
txtstream.WriteLine("    FONT-SIZE: 10px;");
txtstream.WriteLine("    text-align: left;");
txtstream.WriteLine("    white-Space: nowrap='nowrap';");
txtstream.WriteLine("    width: 100%;");
txtstream.WriteLine("}");
txtstream.WriteLine("input");
txtstream.WriteLine("{");
txtstream.WriteLine("    BORDER-RIGHT: #999999 3px solid;");
txtstream.WriteLine("    PADDING-RIGHT: 3px;");
txtstream.WriteLine("    PADDING-LEFT: 3px;");
txtstream.WriteLine("    FONT-WEIGHT: Bold;");
txtstream.WriteLine("    PADDING-BOTTOM: 3px;");
txtstream.WriteLine("    COLOR: white;");
txtstream.WriteLine("    PADDING-TOP: 3px;");
txtstream.WriteLine("    BORDER-BOTTOM: #999 1px solid;");
txtstream.WriteLine("    BACKGROUND-COLOR: navy;");
txtstream.WriteLine("    FONT-FAMILY:  Cambria, serif;");
txtstream.WriteLine("    FONT-SIZE: 12px;");
txtstream.WriteLine("    text-align: left;");
txtstream.WriteLine("    display: table-cell;");
txtstream.WriteLine("    white-Space: nowrap='nowrap';");
txtstream.WriteLine("    width: 100%;");
txtstream.WriteLine("}");
txtstream.WriteLine("h1 {");
txtstream.WriteLine("color: antiquewhite;");
txtstream.WriteLine("text-shadow: 1px 1px 1px black;");
txtstream.WriteLine("padding: 3px;");
txtstream.WriteLine("text-align: center;");
txtstream.WriteLine("box-shadow: inset 2px 2px 5px rgba(0,0,0,0.5), inset -2px -2px 5px rgba(255,255,255,0.5);");
txtstream.WriteLine("}");
txtstream.WriteLine("</style>");
```

www.ingramcontent.com/pod-product-compliance
Lightning Source LLC
Chambersburg PA
CBHW070849070326
40690CB00009B/1769